OCEAN CREATURES
A SPOTTER'S GUIDE

EARTHAWARE
KIDS

Written by: Sabrina Weiss
Illustrated by: Lisa Alderson and Fiona Osbaldstone

EARTHAWARE
KIDS

Copyright © EarthAware Kids, 2024

Published by EarthAware Kids

Created by Weldon Owen Children's Books
A subsidiary of Insight International, L.P.
PO Box 3088
San Rafael, CA 94912
www.insighteditions.com

Weldon Owen Children's Books
Senior Designer: Emma Randall
Senior Editor: Pauline Savage

Insight Editions
Publisher: Raoul Goff
Senior Production Manager: Greg Steffen

ISBN: 979-8-88674-075-2

Manufactured in China.
First printing, July 2024 DRM0724
28 27 26 25 24 5 4 3 2 1

MIX
Paper | Supporting
responsible forestry
FSC® C188448

OCEAN
CREATURES

A SPOTTER'S GUIDE

SABRINA WEISS

CONTENTS

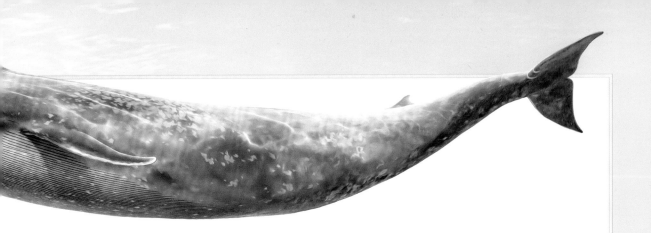

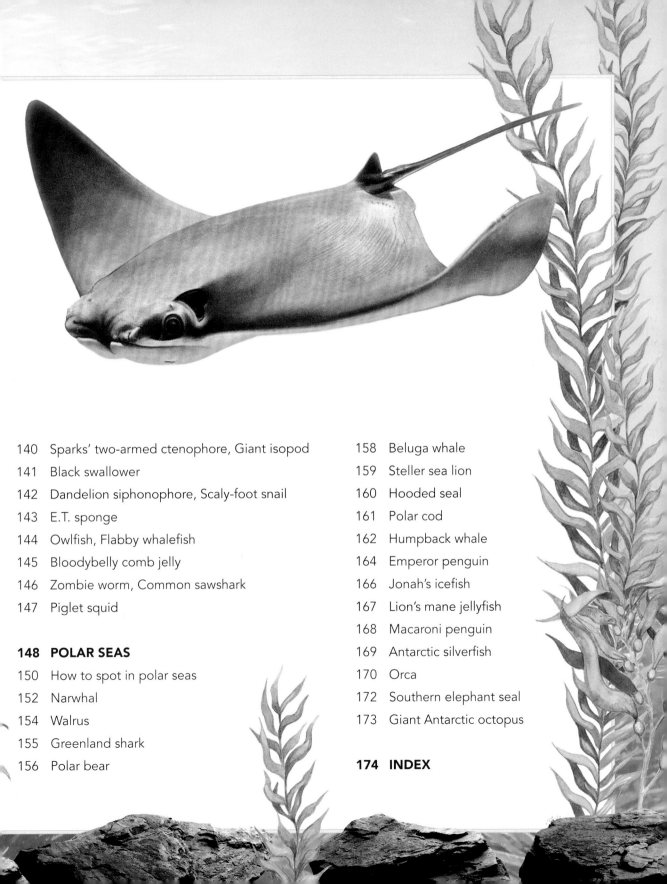

WELCOME TO THE OCEAN

Picture this—you've just dived into the big blue ocean. Ahead of you, a leatherback turtle glides past. Looking down, you see a hermit crab scuttling around on the sandy bottom. Is that a gray seal poking its nose through the swaying leaves?

What will you see on your imaginary ocean adventure?

Gray seal

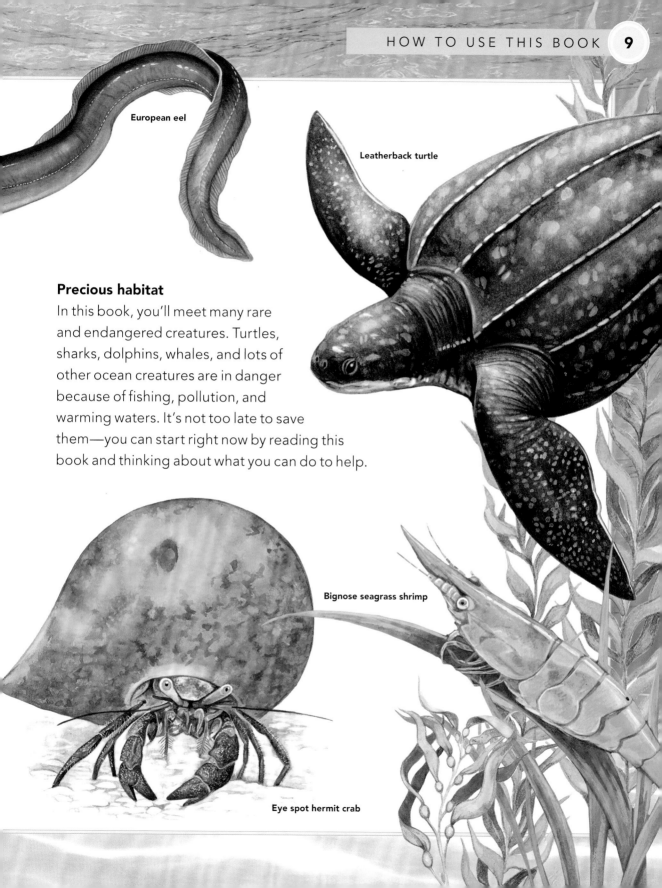

European eel

Leatherback turtle

Precious habitat

In this book, you'll meet many rare and endangered creatures. Turtles, sharks, dolphins, whales, and lots of other ocean creatures are in danger because of fishing, pollution, and warming waters. It's not too late to save them—you can start right now by reading this book and thinking about what you can do to help.

Bignose seagrass shrimp

Eye spot hermit crab

IN THE OCEAN

Turn the pages of this book to discover how to spot all kinds of creatures. Imagine that you are really there, snorkeling and diving through the oceans. Water covers nearly three-quarters of Earth's surface. It is divided into five oceans.

Australian sea lion

Indo-Pacific
This region stretches from the Indian Ocean to the western and central Pacific Ocean. It is home to many creatures.

Arctic Ocean
The Arctic Ocean is the smallest ocean. It surrounds the North Pole. Much of the water freezes over in winter.

Pacific Ocean
The Pacific Ocean is not only the deepest but also the largest of the oceans. It covers around one-third of Earth's surface.

ARCTIC OCEAN

NORTH AMERICA

EUROPE

MEDITERRANEAN SEA

SOUTH ASIA

PACIFIC OCEAN

CENTRAL AMERICA

AFRICA

INDO-PACIFIC

CARIBBEAN SEA

EQUATOR

SOUTHEAST ASIA

PACIFIC OCEAN

SOUTH AMERICA

ATLANTIC OCEAN

INDIAN OCEAN

AUSTRALIA

SOUTHERN OCEAN

Atlantic Ocean
The Atlantic Ocean has very strong currents. These help move warmth around the planet.

Southern Ocean
The Southern Ocean is very cold and windy, which makes it a difficult place to live. The waves get very big here.

Indian Ocean
The warmest waters are usually in the Indian Ocean, especially near the equator.

SPOTTING CREATURES

Follow these simple steps and you will become an expert at spotting ocean creatures in no time.

1 Start by looking up your favorite creatures in the index on page 174. Each one in the book has an entry.

2 Study the detailed artworks. Arrows point to special features.

3 Look out for interesting facts in the colored circles. There are WILD facts at the bottom of some pages, too.

Lionfish

SPOTTER FACT

Lionfish cause harm to reefs in the Caribbean, as they eat the fish that keep the corals healthy.

4 Find where you are on the map. See what kinds of waters the creatures live in.

5 The numbers of many creatures are decreasing. Check here to see how close they are to becoming extinct.

6 Compare the size of the creature with the size of a human.

Fanning out the fins helps the lionfish to corner prey.

Intertidal spider

WHERE IN THE WORLD?

LIVES: native to Indo-Pacific, introduced into western North Atlantic Ocean, Caribbean Sea, and Gulf of Mexico

EATS: fish, mollusks, shrimp and other crustaceans, and invertebrates

STATUS:
🍃 least concern

HOW BIG?

12–15in (30–38cm) long

IT'S WILD! Scientists have discovered at least 240,000 ocean species so far, but there might be around two million more.

CORAL REEFS

HOW TO SPOT IN CORAL REEFS

Dive into the warm, shallow waters, where thousands of corals form stunning reefs. Look at all those colors, shapes, and sizes! A reef is like an underwater city teeming with life—from nibbling parrotfish and stinging anemones to fish that live in pairs or hide in the reef's cracks and crevices.

WHAT IS A CORAL REEF?

LIVING CREATURES Corals are made up of little soft-bodied creatures called polyps.

DIFFERENT SHAPES AND SIZES Corals can look like stones, fans, brains, thorns ... the list is endless!

COLONIES The polyps connect to one another and live in groups called colonies. Some corals form a hard skeleton that links them together.

REEFS When different types of coral colonies join together, they form a reef. Coral reefs grow very slowly and some are thousands of years old.

Use your senses
Imagine you're exploring the most beautiful coral reef, hoping to spot a queen parrotfish. Look and listen—you might be lucky!

Follow the sound
Some creatures make sounds underwater. You can hear the parrotfish munching as it eats.

Notice the mouth
Some fish have unusually shaped mouths. You can tell this is a parrotfish because it has a mouth that looks like a parrot's beak.

Study the body shape
A long, sleek body helps fish zip through coral reefs. Check the color of the scales to know which fish it is.

Queen parrotfish

What spotters need

With lots of bright sunshine and clear waters, you'll be able to see corals and fish just by floating still on the surface of the ocean. A mask and snorkel allow you to see and breathe while swimming underwater. Explore a bit deeper by diving down using an oxygen tank.

CORAL REEF WATCH

Imagine snorkeling in Australia's Great Barrier Reef—the largest coral reef in the world. A local guide can find different fish and make sure you swim safely, avoiding sharp corals and stinging anemones.

Standing out

Fish recognize each other by their bright colors. Moorish idols have yellow, black, and white bodies. They live in pairs.

Stinging tentacles

Creatures that always stay in the same spot, like sea anemones, use wiggly tentacles to sting and catch their food.

Hard corals

The hard skeletons of corals, like in this common sea fan, provide homes and hiding places for lots of other ocean creatures.

WHERE IN THE WORLD?

LIVES: shallow waters in Indo-Pacific

EATS: plankton and nutrients from algae

STATUS: vulnerable

HOW BIG?

4ft (1.2m) long

GIANT CLAM

This massive clam is literally part of the reef, attaching itself to coral or the sandy bottom. Every clam has a unique and colorful shell—no two look the same. As you swim by, the giant clam will slowly close its shell to protect itself.

The soft inside of the clam is called the mantle. It contains algae, which provides food for the clam.

Corals grow on the shell because the clam stays in the same place all its life.

Giant clam

IN DANGER!

Sadly, people take giant clams from the ocean. They sell their pretty shells or keep them in aquariums.

LIONFISH

A stripy lionfish waving its long, fanlike fins is a magnificent sight. Don't let its beauty fool you. This fish is a fierce predator. The lionfish has 18 venomous spines on its back and fins that can give you a painful sting. You'll find it cruising around the reef both night and day. Be sure to stay well away!

WHERE IN THE WORLD?

LIVES: native to Indo-Pacific, introduced into western North Atlantic Ocean, Caribbean Sea, and Gulf of Mexico

EATS: fish, mollusks, shrimp, and other crustaceans and invertebrates

STATUS:

🔖 least concern

HOW BIG?

12–15in (30–38cm) long

The spines stick out like a mane, which is why it's called a lionfish.

The lionfish mostly swallows its prey whole in a lightning-quick strike.

 SPOTTER FACT

Lionfish cause harm to reefs in the Caribbean, as they eat the fish that keep the corals healthy.

Fanning out the fins helps the lionfish to corner its prey.

Lionfish

IT'S WILD!   The lionfish isn't a fussy eater. It snaps up pretty much anything it can find.

STONEFISH

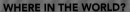

WHERE IN THE WORLD?

LIVES: Indo-Pacific

EATS: small fish, and shrimp and other crustaceans

STATUS:
 least concern

HOW BIG?

10½in (27cm) long

It's hard to spot a stonefish because it looks just like the coral and rocks around it. The stonefish has many venomous spines and is one of the most dangerous fish for humans.

The stonefish stays completely still, waiting to ambush passing prey.

Stonefish

ZEBRA SHARK

When you look at a zebra shark you see spots, not stripes. So why the name? It's because the zebra shark is born with stripes, but these change to spots when it grows up.

WHERE IN THE WORLD?

LIVES: Indo-Pacific

EATS: small fish, mollusks, and crustaceans

STATUS:
 endangered

HOW BIG?

8ft (2.5m) long

Zebra shark

Zebra sharks can swim far from their reef home—sometimes more than 1,200 miles (2,000km) away.

Sea slugs breathe mainly using feathery gills at the back of their body. They can also breathe through their skin.

DON'T MISS!
There are thousands of kinds of sea slug in many shapes and dazzling colors. See how many you can spot!

Two rod-shaped tentacles are used to smell and taste.

Sea slug

The underside of a sea slug's body is called a foot.

WHERE IN THE WORLD?

LIVES: waters around Tonga

EATS: sponges, corals, anemones, and fish eggs

STATUS:
🍃 unknown

HOW BIG?

up to 2in (5cm)

SEA SLUG

On the reef lives a tiny, slimy creature, no bigger than your thumb. Like a land slug, the sea slug has a soft body and no shell. It slides along in search of corals and sponges that it can scrape off the reef to eat. This type of sea slug is called a reticulated goniobranchus. You can recognize it by its reddish-brown spots

IT'S WILD! The sea slug's bright colors warn predators that it's poisonous and dangerous to eat.

LIVES: Indian and Pacific oceans

EATS: algae, sponges, and other invertebrates

STATUS:
least concern

HOW BIG?

8– 9in (21–23cm) long

MOORISH IDOL

You'll often see two stripy fish with a very long trailing back fins swimming together on the reef. They may look almost identical—but you're not seeing double! When a Moorish idol finds a partner, the pair stay together for a while.

The body is flat like a disk.

Moorish idols are white with black stripes and yellow patches.

The long fin on the back helps the fish to stay upright in the water.

The female Moorish idol is slightly bigger than the male.

The long snout can reach food in cracks and crevices in the reef.

DON'T MISS!

Keep a lookout for young Moorish idols swimming together in a big group.

Moorish idol

The fish has a small mouth, so it can only eat algae and tiny creatures.

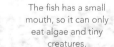

SAND TIGER SHARK

It's easy to tell the sand tiger shark apart from other sharks. It has jagged teeth that stick out in all directions, even when its mouth is closed. Have you noticed it coming to the surface to take a mouthful of air? The shark isn't breathing but sucking the air down into its stomach. This allows it to float without moving as it scans the reef looking for a tasty meal.

WHERE IN THE WORLD?

LIVES: Atlantic, Pacific, and Indian oceans

EATS: fish, rays, squid, crabs, and lobsters

STATUS:
🌿 critically endangered

HOW BIG?

6½–10ft (2–3m) long

Even though it looks fierce, this shark is not aggressive.

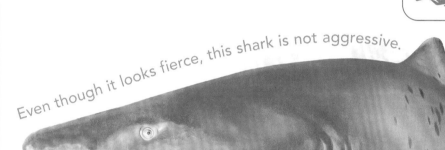

The snout is shaped like a flattened cone.

IN DANGER!
Sand tiger sharks have very few pups. This means there aren't very many of them in the ocean.

This shark stays near to shore and swims close to the ocean floor.

Sand tiger shark

IT'S WILD! This shark loses around 13,000 teeth in its lifetime. It grows new ones as replacements.

WHERE IN THE WORLD?

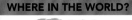

LIVES: Indo-Pacific

EATS: plankton, algae, worms, small crustaceans, and scraps the anemone leaves behind

STATUS:
🖊 least concern

HOW BIG?

2¼–4¼in
(7–11cm) long

COMMON CLOWNFISH

Peek into the stinging tentacles of a carpet anemone and you're likely to find a family of clownfish. These colorful little fish are usually busy keeping their home clean. They eat the anemone's leftover food and pick parasites from its body.

DON'T MISS!

Look for clownfish in family groups. The head of the family is always female, and she is the largest fish.

The female clownfish lays her eggs on rocks near the carpet anemone, safe from predators.

Many types of clownfish have three bold white stripes around their bodies.

Common clownfish

A slimy layer over the skin protects the clownfish from the anemone's stings.

The carpet anemone's tentacles can sting. This keeps predators away.

QUEEN PARROTFISH

If you hear a crackling sound, it's probably a queen parrotfish nibbling on rocks and dead coral. The parrotfish is eating algae, which grows all over the coral reef. By munching all day, the parrotfish helps keep the reef clean and the corals stay healthy.

WHERE IN THE WORLD?

LIVES: Caribbean Sea

EATS: algae and plants

STATUS:
🌿 least concern

HOW BIG?

24in (61cm) long

Parrotfish are usually born female. The fish can become male later in life.

The marking above the queen parrotfish's eye looks like a crown.

The blue-green color shows that this is an adult male. Females and young males are reddish-brown.

SPOTTER FACT

Parrotfish have about 1,000 teeth joined together in 15 rows. These strong teeth can cut through rock.

Queen parrotfish

The parrotfish's teeth look like the beak of a parrot.

IT'S WILD! Parrotfish sleep in a large bubble made of their own slime to keep safe.

WHERE IN THE WORLD?

LIVES: Indo-Pacific

EATS: fish

STATUS:
least concern

HOW BIG?

2¼–6in (6–16cm) long

GEOGRAPHY CONE SNAIL

Have you ever seen a shell with such beautiful patterns? Beware—this shell belongs to one of the most venomous creatures on Earth! The geography cone snail has a long tube called a proboscis that can shoot a powerful venom into its prey. The snail then swallows the fish whole.

As it's a slow mover, the only way the snail can catch fish is to paralyze them with its venom.

This snail hunts at night when fish are resting.

The proboscis looks a bit like a worm. Unsuspecting fish try to eat it, but receive a deadly sting.

The snail sticks out a long tube called a siphon to find food around it.

Geography cone snail

SPOTTER FACT

The snail's venom contains hundreds of different toxins. It is strong enough to kill a human.

BLACKTIP REEF SHARK

A gray fin with a black tip sticking out of the water can only mean one thing—a blacktip reef shark is patrolling the coral reef below. You're safe, though, because it's easily frightened off. This shark is very shy and is just looking for a fishy meal.

Black-tipped fins
This shark gets its name because almost all of the fins on its body have a black tip.

A blacktip reef shark can live for about 15 years.

Blacktip reef sharks hunt both during the day and at night.

Blacktip reef shark

The white belly makes it hard to see the shark from below because it is camouflaged against the bright ocean surface.

WHERE IN THE WORLD?

LIVES: Indo-Pacific

EATS: fish, crustaceans, octopuses, squid, and other mollusks

STATUS:
🐟 vulnerable

HOW BIG?

6ft (1.8m) long

IN DANGER!

Warming oceans are harming coral reefs. That means this shark is losing its home and food.

TASSELLED WOBBEGONG

Take care not to disturb this shark as you dive down to the sandy bottom. You might not even spot it. The tasselled wobbegong lies very still, well camouflaged against the sand. It waits for a fish to come by. Then, SNAP! The shark swallows the fish in the blink of an eye.

WHERE IN THE WORLD?

LIVES: shallow waters around northern Australia and New Guinea

EATS: fish, octopuses, crabs, and lobsters

STATUS: least concern

HOW BIG?

4ft (1.2m) long

When it wants to attract prey, the shark wiggles the tip of its tail to look like a small fish.

Tasselled wobbegong

SPOTTER FACT

The tasselled wobbegong has a very wide mouth. It can eat fish that are almost its own size.

The frilly tassels around the shark's head help to disguise its shape.

IT'S WILD! The shark's tassels are special whiskers called barbels. They help the shark to sense prey.

IN DANGER!

Hawksbill turtles are protected by law to stop people selling their beautiful shells.

A turtle's shell is called a carapace. This hard covering protects the turtle from predators.

Overlapping scales make the edge of the shell look wavy.

Hawksbill turtle

The shell is a swirl of red, orange, brown, and gold colors. This pattern is known as tortoiseshell.

The beak can pry out sponges to eat from crevices in the reef.

HAWKSBILL TURTLE

If you see a sea turtle with a mouth that looks like a bird's beak, it's a hawksbill. This sharp, pointed mouth helps the hawksbill turtle get to food in the narrow spaces between the corals and rocks. A resting turtle can stay underwater for several hours.

WHERE IN THE WORLD?

LIVES: warm waters

EATS: sponges, algae, seagrass, soft corals, mollusks, jellyfish, sea urchins, small fish, and various invertebrates

STATUS:
critically endangered

HOW BIG?

30–35in (75–90cm) long

IT'S WILD! The hawksbill turtle is one of seven species of sea turtle.

ATLANTIC NURSE SHARK

LIVES: eastern and western Atlantic Ocean

EATS: crabs, lobsters, shrimp, sea urchins, squid, octopuses, snails, and fish

STATUS: vulnerable

HOW BIG?

10ft (3m) long

If you see a nurse shark dragging its snout over the sandy ocean floor, that's because it's hungry. This shark has special feelers to search for food hiding in the sand at night. During the day, peek under a coral ledge to see the nurse shark sleeping. It loves to lie and take naps, hidden away.

Adult nurse sharks are yellowy-brown and are sometimes covered in small dark spots.

The tail fin on a nurse shark is elongated.

Atlantic nurse shark

The shark pushes its fins against the sand to turn.

IN DANGER!

People are helping to increase the number of nurse sharks by limiting how many can be fished.

IT'S WILD! Nurse sharks have a good sense of smell. They can find food even in dark water.

WHERE IN THE WORLD?

LIVES: Indo-Pacific

EATS: small fish and invertebrates such as shrimps

STATUS:
near threatened

HOW BIG?

28in (70cm) long

CORAL CATSHARK

You'll have to snorkel at dusk to spot the coral catshark. It hides all day in the nooks and crannies of the reef, then slips out at night to hunt.

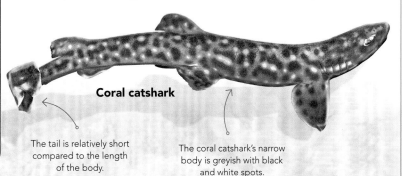

Coral catshark

The tail is relatively short compared to the length of the body.

The coral catshark's narrow body is greyish with black and white spots.

EPAULETTE SHARK

No, your eyes aren't deceiving you—this shark can walk on land! It can stay out of the water for up to two hours.

WHERE IN THE WORLD?

LIVES: shallow, warm waters around Australia and New Guinea

EATS: small fish, crabs, and worms

STATUS:
least concern

HOW BIG?

3ft (1m) long

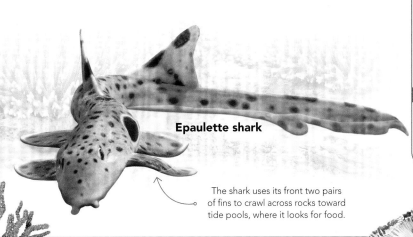

Epaulette shark

The shark uses its front two pairs of fins to crawl across rocks toward tide pools, where it looks for food.

HARLEQUIN SHRIMP

Whenever you see the eye-catching harlequin shrimp, it'll probably be munching on a sea star. These small creatures eat nothing else. The shrimp flips the sea star upside down so that it can get to the softest flesh, usually beginning with its feet.

WHERE IN THE WORLD?

LIVES: Indian and Pacific oceans

EATS: sea stars

STATUS: unknown

HOW BIG?

up to 2in (5cm) long

DON'T MISS!

These shrimp mate for life, so look out for pairs together. The female is slightly bigger than the male.

The antennae on the shrimp's head help it to smell nearby sea stars.

Harlequin shrimp

The shrimp moves slowly using two legs on each side. Luckily, its sea star prey moves even more slowly.

The front claws are flat and large in comparison to the rest of the body.

GUINEAFOWL PUFFER

You're watching an ordinary-looking fish swimming slowly along the reef when suddenly it puffs up into a big, round ball. How? By filling its belly with lots of water. And why? To scare away other fish that want to eat it. It's difficult for predators to swallow a puffed-up fish.

Countless white spots cover the fish's body, including its fins.

The fish inflates within a few seconds to defend itself.

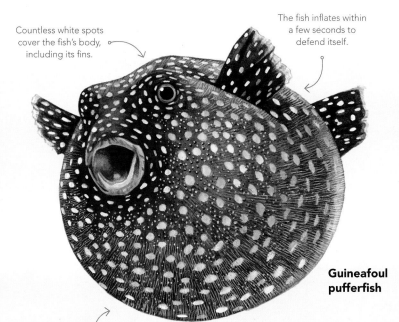

Guineafoul pufferfish

DON'T MISS!
Some guineafowl puffers have different colors. Try to find one that is yellow with black spots.

When the puffer is ready to deflate, strong belly muscles push the water back out of the fish's mouth.

Normal size
When it's uninflated, the guineafowl puffer's body is rectangular and its snout is short.

BRAIN CORAL

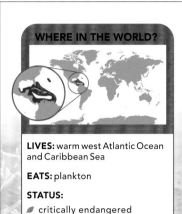

LIVES: warm west Atlantic Ocean and Caribbean Sea

EATS: plankton

STATUS:
🌿 critically endangered

HOW BIG?

6ft (1.8m) wide

Corals don't have brains. But some look like a human brain because they're round, with twisted folds. It's no surprise these are called brain corals. These amazing structures can live for up to 900 years.

The outer layer is alive. The inside is a rock-hard skeleton.

Brain coral

BUBBLE CORAL

Swim in the shallows during the day to see the puffy, pearl-colored bubble coral. At night, these bubbles, or vesicles, shrink. They make space for tentacles that come out to seek food.

During the day, the water-filled vesicles soak up sunlight, which helps the coral grow.

WHERE IN THE WORLD?

LIVES: Indo-Pacific

EATS: plankton

STATUS:
🌿 near threatened

HOW BIG?

up to 16in (40cm) wide

Bubble coral

COMMON SEA FAN

Can you see that purple, treelike structure gently swaying in the water? It has a trunk and many branches just like trees do, but it's really a creature called a sea fan. These amazing fans are related to the corals that build reefs. They gently fan the water to bring food their way.

WHERE IN THE WORLD?

LIVES: western Atlantic Ocean and Caribbean Sea

EATS: plankton

STATUS:
🍃 unknown

HOW BIG?

5ft (1.5m) tall

Like many corals, sea fans have algae inside them that make food using sunlight.

The sea fan anchors itself to hard surfaces such as the rocky ocean floor.

Small, feathery tentacles capture plankton and other bits of food from the water.

DON'T MISS!

When you spot a sea fan, look out for the small fish, snails, and seahorses that like to hide inside it.

Common sea fan

IT'S WILD! Not only do algae make food for the sea fan, they also give the fan its bright purple color.

LIVES: Indian and Pacific oceans

EATS: small fish, crustaceans such as shrimp, mussels, sea urchins, and plankton

STATUS:
🌿 unknown

HOW BIG?

12–20in (30–50cm) long

MAGNIFICENT SEA ANEMONE

Sea anemones are called the flowers of the ocean. Make no mistake—they are living creatures. The magnificent anemone's tentacles look like a soft rug or carpet, but when a fish brushes past them—OUCH! The tentacles sting, paralyzing the fish so that it can no longer swim away.

DON'T MISS!

Dive down 160ft (50m) to find the biggest anemones. They grow together in large groups called colonies.

The tentacles are about 3in (7cm) long. They pull food into the anemone's mouth.

This is the second-largest sea anemone in the world. Only the Mertens' carpet sea anemone is bigger.

The anemone's body sticks to hard surfaces. Its purple color is what gives this anemone its name.

Magnificent sea anemone

WHERE IN THE WORLD?

LIVES: Caribbean Sea

EATS: plankton

STATUS:
🌿 critically endangered

HOW BIG?

up to 6ft (1.8m) wide;
4ft (1.2m) tall

STAGHORN CORAL

Staghorn corals have been around for a very long time—50 million years, to be exact! For the last two million years, these golden corals have been the main builders of coral reefs. New groups, or colonies, form when one of the branches falls off and reattaches itself to the reef.

Staghorn corals don't move. They use tentacles to sting and grab tiny creatures called zooplankton that drift past in the water.

IN DANGER!

People are planting staghorn corals in places where they were once plentiful. This helps the reefs to grow again.

The branches grow 4–8in (10–20cm) every year.

The staghorn coral gets its name because of the way its branches spread outward like a male deer's antlers.

Staghorn coral

IT'S WILD! The staghorn is a nighttime predator. Its tentacles can detect food in the dark.

COASTAL WATERS

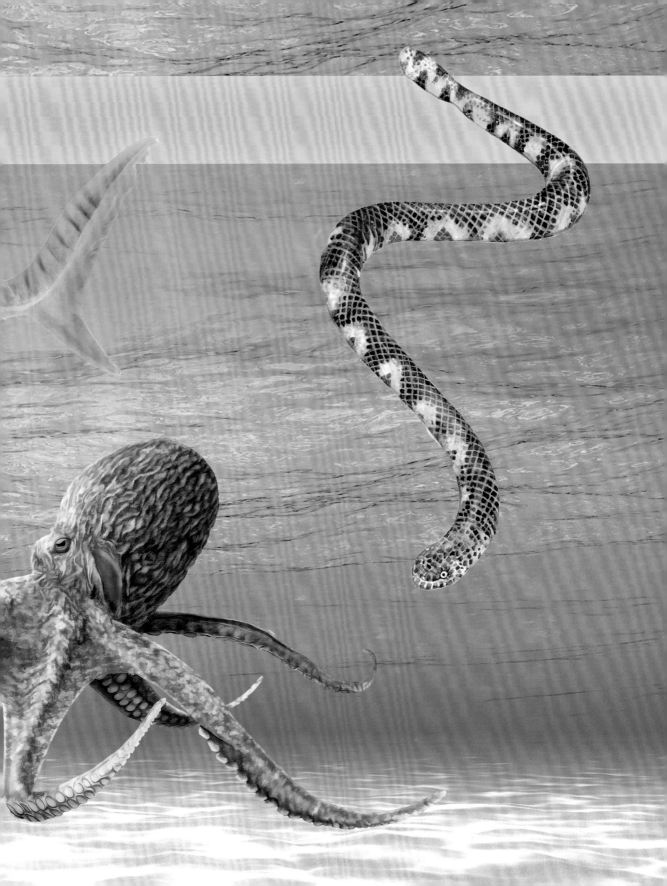

HOW TO SPOT IN COASTAL WATERS

Look! Near the coast, the ocean is full of creatures. Calm, sheltered bays provide a safe haven for rays, dolphins, and fish—especially young ones. They need to grow before they can swim out to the open seas. Close to the shore, there is plenty of food, so even land animals like the marine iguana take to the water.

Notice the stinger
Many creatures have a stinger to protect themselves from predators. This tail can deliver a venomous sting if the ray feels threatened or is stepped on.

Blue-spotted ribbontail ray

Watch the tides
Some creatures shelter in rocky reefs until the tide is high and the water is deep enough for them to swim in. Others appear on the shore at low tide.

Look out for movement
When swimming, the fins of a ray move in a wavelike motion, allowing it to glide gracefully through the water.

Study the seabed
Rays like to lie on the sand. If you can see lots of blue spots on its top, you might be looking at a blue-spotted ribbontail ray.

On the shore
Some coastal creatures spend part of their time on the shore. The marine iguana is a good ocean swimmer, but it makes its home on land.

Marine iguana

WHAT ARE COASTAL WATERS?

LAND MEETS THE OCEAN Coastal waters begin at the shoreline. The water is usually less than 660ft (200m) deep.

RIVERS MEET THE OCEAN The area where freshwater rivers and salty seawater mix is called an estuary. The water is green and cloudy.

TIDES The ocean tide comes in and out, usually twice a day. Creatures that live on the shore have to survive in both dry and wet conditions.

RICH FEEDING GROUNDS Coastal waters are full of nutrients. Here, the ocean is brimming with creatures of all kinds as they come to find food.

Bottlenose dolphin

Breachers
Creatures often jump out of the water, or breach—sometimes to escape predators. A dolphin might breach to tell the others in its pod where to find fish.

What spotters need
Have a notebook with you so that you can jot down what you see on the shore. Then take a boat along the coast. You can spot creatures jumping out of the water from here. Dive down using scuba gear to look for creatures on the seabed.

COASTAL WATERS WATCH
Imagine taking a real trip along the coast. Keep looking carefully around the boat—many creatures are curious and like to swim up close. Birds circling over the water can tell you where schools of fish are.

Bottom dwellers
Some fish wait on the bottom until something to eat appears. The butterfly blenny blends into the sand with its brown-and-gray body.

Butterfly blenny

GREAT HAMMERHEAD SHARK

WHERE IN THE WORLD?

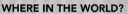

LIVES: warm and cool waters

EATS: fish and crustaceans

STATUS:
🍃 critically endangered

HOW BIG?

13ft (4m) long

There's no mistaking the great hammerhead shark. Can you see how its huge, strange-looking head is shaped like a hammer? This is how it gets its name. The great hammerhead is the biggest of the nine hammerhead species. It roams the coastlines for hundreds of miles in search of food.

There is an eye on either side of the hammerhead's wide head. These allow it to see a large area around itself.

Special sensors in the shark's head detect the electrical fields given off by other ocean creatures.

This shark's large size means it has no predators in the ocean.

Great hammerhead shark

IN DANGER!

People like to eat shark fins. Sadly, this means that too many of these amazing sharks are being caught.

BOX JELLYFISH

If you ever spot a box-shaped creature with long tentacles, give it plenty of space. It's likely to be a box jellyfish—one of the world's most venomous creatures. Its tentacles contain powerful stinging cells. These stings are why the box jellyfish is also known as the sea wasp.

WHERE IN THE WORLD?

LIVES: Indo-Pacific

EATS: fish, worms, and crustaceans

STATUS:
🍃 unknown

HOW BIG?

bell 8in (20cm) wide; tentacles up to 10ft (3m) long

This jellyfish gets its name from its box-shaped body, or bell.

The blue, almost see-through color makes the box jellyfish difficult to spot.

SPOTTER FACT

The box jellyfish has a group of six eyes on each side of its square body. That's 24 eyes altogether!

Box jellyfish

There are up to 60 tentacles—about 15 on each corner of the body. Each tentacle has about 5,000 stinging cells.

IT'S WILD! Most jellyfish just drift with the ocean current, but the box jellyfish is a strong swimmer.

SPINY LOBSTER

During the day, this colorful lobster hides in crevices. Find it at night in sandy or muddy areas, close to where rivers meet the ocean.

When threatened, the lobster points its two large antennae forward to protect itself.

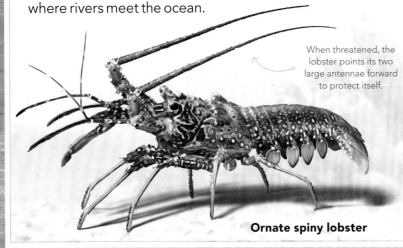

Ornate spiny lobster

WHERE IN THE WORLD?

LIVES: Indo-Pacific

EATS: small crustaceans, slugs, snails, and plants

STATUS: least concern

HOW BIG?

14in (35cm) long

WHERE IN THE WORLD?

LIVES: North Pacific Ocean

EATS: crab, lobster, shrimp, clams, and fish

STATUS: least concern

HOW BIG?

16ft (5m) long

GIANT PACIFIC OCTOPUS

The giant Pacific octopus is a supermom. When she lays her eggs, she protects them by gently wrapping her arms around them. Many creatures eat octopus eggs, so she will guard her clutch for months until they hatch. You might catch a glimpse of her swirling around in the water and shooing predators away.

Special cells on its arms allow the octopus to taste things. This prevents it from eating poisonous fish.

WHERE IN THE WORLD?

LIVES: warm and cool waters

EATS: almost anything, including fish, other sharks, sea turtles, mollusks, seabirds, and garbage

STATUS:
 near threatened

HOW BIG?

18ft (5.5m) long

TIGER SHARK

Have you noticed the stripes that cover this shark's body from top to bottom? They're like the markings of a tiger, but in gray. That's how this shark gets its name.

Tiger shark

The tiger shark is one of the biggest sharks. It is a fearsome hunter.

The head is large and bulbous. The octopus's mouth is underneath its head, at the base of its arms. It is like a hard beak.

SPOTTER FACT

This is the biggest octopus in the world, but it can squeeze its body through a hole the size of a lemon.

Giant Pacific octopus

The octopus has about 250 suction cups on each of its eight arms. These help it anchor itself or hold on to prey.

BASKING SHARK

In the distance looms a mouth so big it could swallow you whole. But don't worry! The basking shark only has an appetite for zooplankton—tiny creatures that float in the ocean. You'll often see this gentle giant swimming near the surface with its mouth wide open. It has to swallow half a million gallons of water each day to get all the food it needs.

WHERE IN THE WORLD?

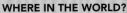

LIVES: Atlantic and Pacific oceans

EATS: krill, small jellyfish, and other zooplankton

STATUS: endangered

HOW BIG?

up to 39ft (12m) long

The large, triangular back fin can be 3ft (1m) tall. It often pokes out of the water.

Although it feeds near the surface, this shark can dive down to 4,000ft (1,200m).

IN DANGER!

Basking sharks are fished for food. There are now laws in many countries to protect them.

Basking shark

The dark parts inside the mouth are gill rakers. They remove tiny creatures called zooplankton from the water.

WHERE IN THE WORLD?

LIVES: waters around North Island of New Zealand

EATS: small fish and squid

STATUS:

▰ critically endangered

HOW BIG?

5ft (1.5m) long

MĀUI DOLPHIN

DON'T MISS!

Look out for this dolphin in harbors along the coast. It likes to feed in shallow or sheltered waters.

This is not only one of the smallest dolphins in the world, it is also the rarest. There are fewer than 50 Māui dolphins left in the wild. You'll find this special creature off the coast of New Zealand, where it lives in small groups, or pods.

Māui dolphins live for about 20 years.

The back fin is rounded. No other dolphin's fin is this shape.

The snout of the Māui dolphin is much shorter than in other dolphin species.

Māui dolphin

IN DANGER!

The biggest danger to the dolphins is getting trapped in fishing nets. More protection is needed to help them.

The tail fluke is large compared to the size of the short, stocky body.

MARINE IGUANA

It's time to warm up before the next swim in the cold waters of the Pacific Ocean! The marine iguana does this by lying on a rock to bask in the sun.

Reptiles are cold-blooded and need the sun to warm their bodies. Dark skin helps the iguana soak up sunlight quickly.

The marine iguana is the only ocean swimmer in the lizard family.

Marine iguana

WHERE IN THE WORLD?

LIVES: Galápagos Islands of Ecuador

EATS: algae

STATUS:
🍃 vulnerable

HOW BIG?

28in (70cm) long

PINK SAND DOLLAR

You're more likely to spot this pink treasure washed up on a beach than in the ocean. That's because when it's in the water, the sand dollar buries itself in the sandy seabed.

Sand dollars are covered in tiny spines. They use these to move along the sand.

Pink sand dollar

WHERE IN THE WORLD?

LIVES: Indo-Pacific

EATS: algae, plankton, and small crustaceans

STATUS:
🍃 unknown

HOW BIG?

4–6in (11–16cm) wide

BOTTLENOSE DOLPHIN

As you sail along the coast, something's following you. It's not another boat, but a bottlenose dolphin. These playful creatures often swim alongside boats for fun. Bottlenose dolphins can travel about 3,000 miles (5,000km) every year in search of food or warmer waters.

SPOTTER FACT
Dolphins "talk" to each other using clicks and whistles. They know what family members sound like, even after years apart.

Bottlenose dolphins can leap as high as 20ft (6m) in the air.

Dolphins generally hunt together in order to catch as many fish as possible. They swallow their prey whole.

The back fin helps the dolphin stay steady in the water, like a boat's keel.

Bottlenose dolphin

WHERE IN THE WORLD?

LIVES: warm and cool waters

EATS: fish, squid, and crustaceans

STATUS:
🖋 least concern

HOW BIG?

8–10ft (2.5–3m) long

SPINY DOGFISH

The spiny dogfish is a type of shark. You can identify it by the row of small white spots on each side. It also has a sharp, venomous spine in front of each of its back fins. When it's threatened, the spiny dogfish arches its back and uses these spines to poke attackers. This shark is called a dogfish because it hunts in groups, like wild dogs do.

WHERE IN THE WORLD?

LIVES: Atlantic and Pacific oceans, and Mediterranean and Black seas

EATS: fish, squid, jellyfish, and crustaceans

STATUS:
🍃 vulnerable

HOW BIG?

28–39in (70–100cm) long

The spines in front of the back fins give a mild sting. This usually sees most predators off.

This shark is usually found in shallow coastal waters. It sometimes dives down to 6,500ft (2,000m).

Spiny dogfish

The spiny dogfish has large eyes and a pointed snout. It bites its prey with sharp teeth.

IN DANGER!

Spiny dogfish are threatened by fishing. The number of them in the ocean is low because they grow so slowly.

EUROPEAN EEL

The European eel has an amazing life cycle. Baby eels are born in the Sargasso Sea in the Caribbean. They drift eastward across the Atlantic Ocean for between seven months and three years to reach the freshwater rivers of Europe. These eels spend most of their time in rivers, only returning to the ocean for the last part of their lives.

DON'T MISS!

Go to a river mouth to see the shimmering, silvery eel as it returns to the ocean.

These eels are born and die in the ocean, but spend up to 20 years in rivers.

The eel has a single pair of fins on its long, snakelike body.

European eel

IN DANGER!

This eel was once very common. There are now much fewer of them because of fishing and dam building.

The eel changes from transparent to yellow-brown when it enters fresh water. It becomes silver near the end of its life.

WHERE IN THE WORLD?

LIVES: Sargasso and Mediterranean seas and eastern Atlantic Ocean

EATS: fish, mollusks, crustaceans, insects, worms, and dead creatures

STATUS:
🐟 critically endangered

HOW BIG?

14in (35cm) long

SPINNER SHARK

A spinner shark on the hunt is a sight not to be missed. This creature speeds through schools of fish while spinning itself around. With its mouth wide open, the shark snaps up fish from all directions. Then, WHOOSH! It ends in a magnificent spinning leap out of the water.

WHERE IN THE WORLD?

LIVES: warm waters of Atlantic Ocean, Indo-Pacific, Gulf of Mexico, and Mediterranean Sea

EATS: fish

STATUS:
vulnerable

HOW BIG?

8ft (2.5m) long

The long, slim body is mostly gray or coppery, with white bands along the sides.

The spinner shark is often mistaken for the blacktip shark because its fins have dark gray or black tips.

Spinner shark

IN DANGER!

The spinner shark is caught by humans for food. It is now under threat of extinction.

Spinner sharks can leap up to 20ft (6m) into the air, spinning around three times.

INTERTIDAL SPIDER

If you walk along the rocky shore where this tiny spider lives, you'll notice that the tide brings in water once or twice a day. To stop itself from getting swept away at high tide, the intertidal spider shelters in empty shells or in burrows dug by worms. It spins a silk web to seal the entrance. This traps air inside and keeps the water out.

DON'T MISS!

Search for the intertidal spider at night. At low tide, it walks over the rocks in search of a meal.

The intertidal spider rests during the day and becomes active at night.

The spider can stay in its watertight shelter for up to 19 days. It survives on the air it has sealed inside.

The fangs are large for the spider's body size.

Intertidal spider

Like all spiders, the intertidal spider has four pairs of walking legs.

WHERE IN THE WORLD?

LIVES: waters around New Zealand and New Caledonia

EATS: Sea lice and other small invertebrates

STATUS:
🦑 unknown

HOW BIG?

⅓in (8mm) long

BULL SHARK

It's wise to stay well away from the ferocious bull shark. This daring ocean predator sometimes ventures into freshwater rivers to hunt for fish. If you stand by a river mouth, you might spot its big back fin sticking out of the water as it glides by.

WHERE IN THE WORLD?

LIVES: warm waters of all oceans

EATS: fish, sea turtles, seals, dolphins, and seabirds

STATUS: vulnerable

HOW BIG?

11ft (3.5m) long

The bull shark's back fin has no markings, unlike many other sharks' fins.

Sharks, whales, and dolphins often have remora fish attached to them. These little fish help to keep their bigger hosts clean.

Bull shark

Bull sharks have long fins on their sides of their stocky bodies.

These sharks can't see very well. They find food by sensing the electric fields around other creatures.

IN DANGER!

People catch bull sharks for their meat, fins, and liver oil. Some countries now have laws to protect them.

IT'S WILD! This shark has a short, blunt snout. It often head-butts its prey before it attacks.

DUBOIS' SEA SNAKE

If you stay very still in the shallows, you might see the Dubois' sea snake slipping past you. Give it plenty of space, because this is one of the most venomous snakes in the world! It will only bite if it feels threatened, and saves its precious venom for its prey.

The flattened, paddlelike tail makes this sea snake a strong swimmer.

Every few weeks, sea snakes shed their skin. This allows them to grow and gets rid of algae and tiny creatures from their bodies.

The Dubois' snake has smooth creamy-white and dark scales. These are arranged in 19 bands across its body.

The snake can stay underwater for up to two hours before coming up for air.

WHERE IN THE WORLD?

LIVES: waters around Australia, New Guinea, and New Caledonia

EATS: moray eels and fish

STATUS:
🔖 least concern

HOW BIG?

3ft (1m) long

Dubois' sea snake

DON'T MISS!

Watch for the sea snake when night falls. It hides around rocky reefs or in sandy seabeds.

IT'S WILD! This snake has one lung that stretches the length of its body. It can also breathe through its skin.

BLUE-SPOTTED RIBBONTAIL RAY

Your best chance of spotting this shy ray is during the rising tide, when it comes out from the rocky reef to look for prey. You'll recognize it from its olive-green oval body, which is covered with blue spots. It also has two blue stripes along its long tail.

WHERE IN THE WORLD?

LIVES: Indo-Pacific

EATS: mollusks, worms, shrimp, crabs, and small fish

STATUS: least concern

HOW BIG?

up to 14in (35cm) wide and 28in (70cm) long

The ray's eyes stick out from its body. Scientists have shown that this helps the ray to swim more efficiently.

Blue-spotted ribbontail ray

The ray's mouth and gills are on the pale underside of its body.

Most of the ray's body is made up of fin. The ray moves its fins in a gentle rippling motion in order to swim.

DON'T MISS!

Look out for the ray in sandy shallows. As it swims, it looks like it's flying through the water.

VELVET CRAB

Keep a lookout along rocky shores for the bright red eyes of this fast-moving crab. Be careful not to bring your fingers anywhere near its front claws. The velvet crab is aggressive and is not afraid to give a nasty pinch whenever it feels threatened.

SPOTTER FACT

The female carries thousands of orange eggs on her underside. This protects them from hungry predators.

All swimming crabs have flattened hind legs, which allow them to move through the water quickly.

The top of the shell, or carapace, is covered in short hairs. These are soft to the touch, like velvet material.

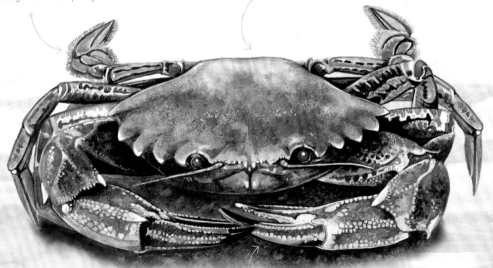

Velvet crab

The two large claws in front of the head are called pincers.

EUROPEAN PLAICE

The European plaice buries itself in sand during the day to keep safe from predators and to surprise its prey. If it weren't for the bright orange spots on its brown top side, you could easily overlook this flat fish. It's harmless, so if you disturb it as you're wading along, it will quickly move to another spot.

WHERE IN THE WORLD?

LIVES: eastern Atlantic Ocean and Mediterranean Sea

EATS: fish, mollusks, crustaceans, and other invertebrates

STATUS: least concern

HOW BIG?

16in (40cm) long

The European plaice belongs to the family of flatfish. It lives on sandy bottoms, gravel, and mud.

The European plaice feeds on creatures that live on the sandy bottom.

European plaice

DON'T MISS!

Look closely! The plaice can hide by changing the color on its back to suit its surroundings.

Unlike other fish, both eyes are on the right side of its body. This means the plaice can see all around when lying in the sand.

BUTTERFLY BLENNY

WHERE IN THE WORLD?

LIVES: Mediterranean Sea, Black Sea, and eastern Atlantic Ocean

EATS: small fish, mollusks and crustaceans

STATUS:
🍃 least concern

HOW BIG?

8in (20cm) long

The best place to see a butterfly blenny is on hard mud or rocky seabeds. During the day, this small fish likes to hide in crevices or under rocks. As soon as it gets dark, it comes out to look for food. Even in the gloom, you'll see it striking a pose, with its back fin standing up tall like a fancy crown. It does this with the help of 11 sharp rays, or spines.

The back fin has a large black spot in the middle.

Butterfly blenny

The back part of the body is much narrower than the front.

Butterfly blennies live alone. They only come together to mate.

The front swimming fins are large and rounded.

SPOTTER FACT

The female blenny lays her eggs in an abandoned shell. The eggs are guarded by the male.

WHALE SHARK

How many white spots can you see on the whale shark's fins and body—100, 1,000, or 10,000? Counting them is impossible, but you could take a photo. That's what scientists do to recognize an individual whale shark. Each of these gentle giants has its own pattern of spots, much like humans have unique fingerprints.

IN DANGER!
Whale sharks are caught on purpose or by accident. That's why there are not many left in the ocean.

One of the shark's back fins is much bigger than the other.

Whale shark

This giant shark feeds near the surface. It eats tiny creatures and plants known as plankton.

The shark moves its tail fin from side to side to swim.

What is plankton?

Tiny creatures such as krill, fish eggs, and young fish are called zooplankton. They are an important food for many ocean species. Zooplankton drift near the surface and feed on phytoplankton, which are little plants that need sunlight to grow.

Zooplankton

Whale sharks can travel huge distances from coast to coast.

The head is broad and flat, and the mouth is huge.

Whale sharks swim with their mouths open. A special filter over the gills traps the food while letting the water out.

Whale sharks are the world's largest fish.

 **DON'T MISS!**

Look for colorful clouds of plankton in the water. These bring whale sharks close to the shore to feed.

WHERE IN THE WORLD?

LIVES: warm waters (except Mediterranean Sea)

EATS: zooplankton such as krill, shrimp, and the eggs and larvae of crabs and fish

STATUS:
endangered

HOW BIG?

up to 60ft (18m) long

KELP FORESTS

HOW TO SPOT IN KELP FORESTS

Peer through the thick, dark forest of kelp to spot playful otters, mysterious cuttlefish, and colorful cuckoo wrasses. Urchins love to munch on the kelp—look for them around the bottom of each tall weed. Sea otters wind themselves in kelp so that they don't float away while they're asleep.

Hiding place
The dense forest is a safe place to lay eggs. Once these cuckoo wrasses have mated, their eggs stay hidden from predators looking for a snack.

Use your senses
Imagine you're exploring a dense kelp forest. It can be quite gloomy here, so keep your eyes peeled and watch out for any tell-tale movements.

Giant cuttlefish

Be careful
Cuttlefish and many other creatures are shy. Make sure you swim slowly and avoid any sudden movements that might surprise them.

Hungry hunters
Sea otters come to kelp forests for their favorite meal—sea urchins. By eating them, the otters keep the numbers of urchins under control.

Study the body
The cuttlefish has a soft body and wiggly things around its mouth. These are its eight arms and two tentacles.

What spotters need

Kelp forests are very dense near the surface because the tallest stipes spread across the top of the water. Dive down at the edge of the forest and enter from there. A dive light and compass will help you find your way on cloudier days.

Look at the coloring

Some creatures can change their color and texture to match their surroundings. The cuttlefish can copy the shades of the kelp.

WHAT IS A KELP FOREST?

UNDERWATER WEED Kelp is not a plant, but algae. It's the largest kind. Kelp uses sunlight and nutrients from the water to grow.

SHALLOW WATER Forests are found in ocean shallows where the sun's rays can still reach.

TALL STIPES Kelp has long, ropelike stems called stipes. Instead of roots, kelp has holdfasts, which anchor each stipe to the rocky ocean floor.

DIFFERENT HOMES Some creatures live on the bladelike leaves. Others rest between the stipes or around the holdfasts.

Many munchers

It's normal to find sea urchins in kelp forests because they love eating the kelp. If there are too many urchins, they might destroy the forest.

KELP FOREST WATCH

Imagine you're in a real kelp forest. See how the tall stipes sway with the current. Look along the leaves, between the stipes, and down toward the holdfasts to spot a whole host of different ocean creatures.

WHERE IN THE WORLD?

LIVES: Pacific coast of North America

EATS: algae, especially kelp

STATUS:
unknown

HOW BIG?

up to 3in (7cm) wide

PURPLE SEA URCHIN

These perfectly round, spiky creatures love to graze on kelp. Dive at night to see them moving around the seabed on their tube feet.

Purple spines cover almost every part of the sea urchin's body. They protect it from predators.

Purple sea urchin

PAJAMA SHARK

To see the pajama shark, you have to wait until it gets dark. During the day, this shy shark rests in caves, beneath rocks, or within the kelp.

This catshark gets its name from these markings. They look like the stripes on old-fashioned pajamas.

WHERE IN THE WORLD?

LIVES: waters around South Africa

EATS: crabs and other crustaceans, small fish, and octopuses

STATUS:
least concern

HOW BIG?

3ft (1m) long

Pajama shark

GRACEFUL DECORATOR CRAB

This little crab is a master of disguise, so you'll need to have a keen eye to spot it. It decorates its shell with algae and small creatures to look like a rock on the kelp forest floor. Without this camouflage, the moving feelers on its head could give the crab away to hungry fish.

WHERE IN THE WORLD?

LIVES: North Pacific Ocean and Bering Sea

EATS: algae, sponges, and plankton

STATUS:
🖋 unknown

HOW BIG?

5in (12cm) wide

There are five long, thin walking legs on each side.

Graceful decorator crab

The shell, or carapace, is shaped like a heart. It is 2in (5cm) long.

This crab has two eyes on stalks and two sets of feelers.

The graceful decorator crab uses its claws for decorating itself, but also for defense.

SPOTTER FACT

The crab's body is covered with lots of tiny hooks to hold sponges, small creatures, or pieces of kelp in place.

WHERE IN THE WORLD?

LIVES: northeast Atlantic Ocean

EATS: fish, squid, and crustaceans

STATUS:
least concern

HOW BIG?

6ft (2m) long

GRAY SEAL

Don't be surprised to find a gray seal swimming alongside you as you snorkel through the water. It has excellent hearing and is probably curious about your splashing. The gray seal can twist and turn like an acrobat as it hunts for food. If it needs to, it can hide from predators in the kelp.

The gray seal's head is longer than the heads of other seals.

The short front flippers help the seal quickly change direction. Each flipper has five claws that can be used to tear food.

Long whiskers help the seal find food in murky water.

Gray seal

SPOTTER FACT

This seal's scientific name means "hook-nosed sea pig." This is because the male has a long, sloping snout.

Gray seals have gray or brown fur with dark spots. Each seal has a different pattern of spots.

GRAY WHALE

A huge gray whale glides gracefully past you. Look how it barely touches the long strands of kelp as it swims slowly along. Gray whales visit kelp forests to find food and hide from predators. They also come here to shelter from storms out at sea.

DON'T MISS!

Look out for a gray whale calf swimming alongside its mother. Kelp forests offer good protection for newborns.

Small creatures called barnacles stick to the whale and stay with it for life.

The end of a whale's tail is called a fluke. A gray whale's fluke is 10ft (3m) wide.

This whale normally swims alone or in small groups.

Gray whale

Inside the mouth are bristly, comblike plates called baleens. These trap food as the whale swallows water.

WHERE IN THE WORLD?

LIVES: North Pacific Ocean

EATS: zooplankton and crustaceans

STATUS:
🍃 least concern

HOW BIG?

up to 50ft (15m) long

GIANT CUTTLEFISH

Prepare for a dazzling display! The giant cuttlefish can change color in an instant. One minute it's flashing pink and purple to attract a mate. The next, it's turned green and is twirling its arms around to look like kelp swaying in the water.

Giant cuttlefish live for just two to four years. Many die after they have mated or laid eggs.

A cuttlefish's body is called a mantle. The giant cuttlefish's mantle can grow up to 20in (50cm) long.

Giant cuttlefish

WHERE IN THE WORLD?

LIVES: waters around Australia

EATS: fish and crustaceans

STATUS:
🍃 near threatened

HOW BIG?

up to 3ft (1m) long

SPOTTER FACT

As well as changing color, cuttlefish can take on different textures to match kelp, rocks, or coral.

There are two feeding tentacles. These are longer than the cuttlefish's arms and bring food to its mouth.

GARIBALDI

It's hard to miss the garibaldi swimming toward you, because of its bright orange color. This male just wants to chase you away from its territory—the area he has made his home. He could also be protecting his nest. Males guard the female's eggs and work to keep the nest clean.

WHERE IN THE WORLD?

LIVES: eastern Pacific Ocean

EATS: algae, small shellfish, sponges, and worms

STATUS:
🍃 least concern

HOW BIG?

14in (35cm) long

A garibaldi's tail fin is heart shaped. Each half of a fish's tail is called a lobe.

This species belongs to the damselfish family.

The fish's diet includes sponges. Scientists think these give the garibaldi its orange color.

Garibaldi

The mouth opening is very small. This makes the lips appear large by comparison.

IT'S WILD! When a male wants to impress a female, he swims round and round in acrobatic loops.

BROADNOSE SEVENGILL SHARK

Sharks take out oxygen from the water in order to breathe. After breathing, the shark lets out water through these gills.

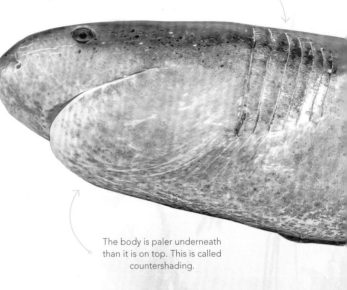

Look at the sides of this shark, where its gill slits are. Most sharks have five gills on each side for breathing, but not this one—it has seven. Do you see its wide snout, too? This explains why this species is called the broadnose sevengill shark.

The body is paler underneath than it is on top. This is called countershading.

SWELL SHARK

Get ready to dive into the mysterious world of the swell shark. When moonlight touches its skin, this shark gives off a greenish glow. Only other swell sharks can see this.

LIVES: eastern Pacific Ocean

EATS: small fish, mollusks, and crustaceans

STATUS:
🍃 least concern

HOW BIG?

3ft (1m) long

Swell shark

The swell shark gets its name because it inflates itself to twice its normal size when threatened.

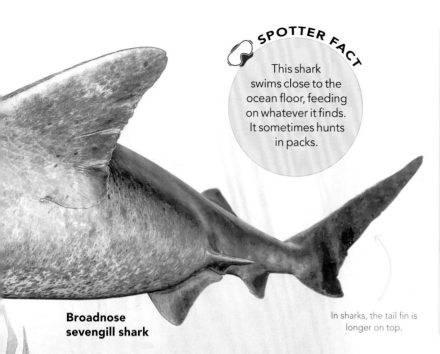

SPOTTER FACT

This shark swims close to the ocean floor, feeding on whatever it finds. It sometimes hunts in packs.

Broadnose sevengill shark

In sharks, the tail fin is longer on top.

WHERE IN THE WORLD?

LIVES: cool coastal waters of Pacific and South Atlantic oceans

EATS: fish, rays, crabs, dolphins, seals, other sharks, and dead creatures

STATUS:
🍃 vulnerable

HOW BIG?

10ft (3m) long

AFRICAN PENGUIN

WHERE IN THE WORLD?

LIVES: waters around southern Africa

EATS: fish

STATUS:
🍃 endangered

HOW BIG?

24–27in (60–68cm) long

The African penguin comes on to land only to breed, shed old feathers, and rest. Most of the time, it's out at sea.

Penguins can't fly, so their wings are used like flippers for swimming.

African penguin

Female cuckoo wrasses are orangey-pink. They have black and white blotches on their backs.

Female cuckoo wrasse

DON'T MISS!

The male wants the female to choose his nest. Watch as his colors grow even brighter to attract her attention.

The female is smaller than the male. She lays about 1,000 eggs in the nest that the male makes.

The male cuckoo wrasse has blue, green, and orange markings.

The shiny, wavy lines stretch the length of the body.

Male cuckoo wrasse

WHERE IN THE WORLD?

LIVES: eastern Atlantic Ocean and Mediterranean Sea

EATS: crustaceans, fish, and mollusks

STATUS:
🍃 least concern

HOW BIG?

females 12in (30cm) long; males up to 16in (40cm) long

female   male

CUCKOO WRASSE

Dive down to the rocky bottom to see the male cuckoo wrasse in action. When it's time to start a family, he builds a nest from small rocks and seaweed. Then he invites a female to lay her eggs. He guards the eggs until they hatch.

IT'S WILD!   Every cuckoo wrasse begins life as a female. Some change into males as they grow.

WEEDY SEADRAGON

WHERE IN THE WORLD?

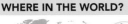

LIVES: waters around southern Australia

EATS: small crustaceans and zooplankton

STATUS:
🍃 least concern

HOW BIG?

18in (46cm) long

Scan the water carefully to spy the weedy seadragon. See how it blends in with the swaying fronds of kelp, thanks to the leaflike fins on its reddish body. This makes the seadragon difficult for predators—and spotters—to find.

The weedy seadragon's leafy fins look like small bits of kelp. These give this creature its name.

The long, thin snout sucks up food into the seadragon's tiny, toothless mouth.

SPOTTER FACT

The female gives her eggs to the male to look after. He carries them under his tail until they hatch.

Unlike their close relative, the seahorse, seadragons can't twist their tails to hold on to things.

This fish swims slowly using the fins on its belly and back. It often just drifts in the water.

Weedy seadragon

KELP SNAIL

LIVES: Pacific coast of North America

EATS: kelp

STATUS: unknown

HOW BIG?

1½in (4cm) long

If you look along a stipe of kelp, you're likely to come across this snail. It eats the kelp, which stops it growing out of control. This keeps the underwater forest healthy.

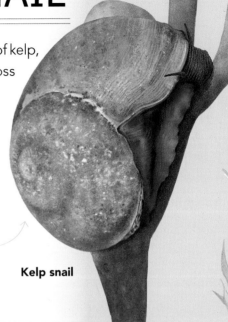

The snail travels up and down the kelp stipes all day as it feeds.

Kelp snail

CHILEAN BASKET STAR

The Chilean basket star is a member of the brittle star family. It usually lives in much deeper water, but sometimes you can see it in the shallows, hanging from kelp.

Five central arms divide into many branches to grab plankton from the water.

WHERE IN THE WORLD?

LIVES: Southern, Atlantic, and Pacific oceans

EATS: plankton

STATUS: unknown

HOW BIG?

up to 8in (20cm) wide

Chilean basket star

RED HANDFISH

Quick, look down! You might just see a red handfish peeking out from under kelp. This fish gets its name because its front fins look like hands. The handfish uses these fins to walk on the ocean floor—it doesn't swim like other fish. Also keep an eye out for this very rare creature near sandy and rocky reefs.

WHERE IN THE WORLD?

LIVES: waters around Tasmania

EATS: small crustaceans and worms

STATUS:
critically endangered

HOW BIG?

3½in (9cm) long

The handfish's body is covered in lots of flattened, wartlike bumps.

The fin on the handfish's head stands up tall.

Red handfish

The female lays eggs at the bottom of kelp strands and guards them until they hatch.

The fish pushes its hand-shaped fins against the bottom to move around.

IT'S WILD! This is one of the rarest fish in the world. There are only about 100 left in the ocean.

AUSTRALIAN SEA LION

Take a trip to Australia if you want to see this rare creature. The Australian sea lion is curious and playful. If you stay completely still in the water, it might come close to you to get a good look.

The flippers are short and narrow. They can be used to walk on land.

The sea lion "talks" using growls, clicks, and barks.

Males are longer than females and three times as heavy. They can weigh up to 550lb (250kg).

Australian sea lion

This type of sea lion has a large head. The snout is short and rounded.

IN DANGER!

These sea lions are protected by law. They are still in danger because they get caught in fishing nets.

SEA OTTER

LIVES: North Pacific Ocean

EATS: sea urchins, clams, and crabs

STATUS:
endangered

HOW BIG?

4ft (1.2m) long

If you see a sea otter sitting on the rocks, it's probably keeping away from underwater predators. Otters spend most of their time in the ocean and are good swimmers.

The tail is short and flattened.

Sea otter

LEOPARD SHARK

WHERE IN THE WORLD?

LIVES: Pacific coast of North America

EATS: crabs, shrimp, clams, octopuses, worms, and fish and their eggs

STATUS:
least concern

HOW BIG?

5¼ft (1.6m) long

Just above the ocean floor lurks a shark you'll easily recognize because of its markings. The leopard shark has a line of large, dark oval bands across its back. It has smaller, round spots on its sides, like a leopard.

The female keeps her eggs inside her body. The baby sharks hatch there and swim out as live young.

Leopard shark

SEAGRASS MEADOWS

HOW TO SPOT IN SEAGRASS MEADOWS

Keep your eyes peeled! Seagrass meadows are a cozy hideout for small creatures that don't want to be found by hungry predators. The swaying grasses themselves make a tasty meal. The meadow is like a big buffet on the ocean floor that attracts many creatures, from gracefully swimming green turtles to small shrimp perching on the leaves.

Search at high tide
Explore seagrass meadows when the tide is in. This is when creatures move here from their hiding spots in nearby reefs.

Notice changing colors
Look for colors and patterns on the octopus that match the seagrass around it. The curled octopus is usually a mix of red, brown, and yellow.

Look out for gentle movements
The curled octopus is well hidden in the seagrass. Watch for movement to help you spot it.

Observe twirling limbs
These arms, often curling and reaching, will tell you that an octopus is there.

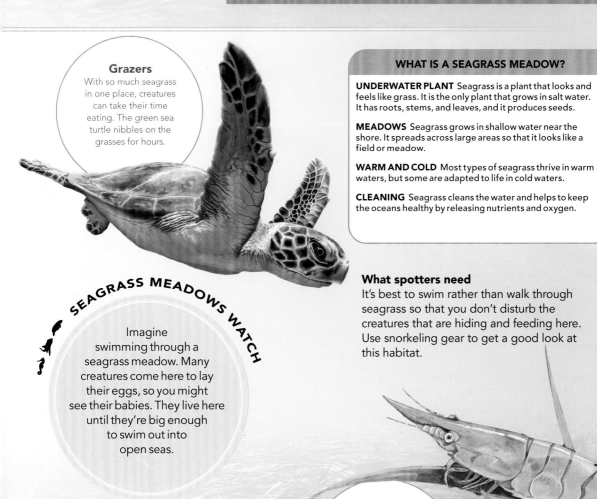

Grazers

With so much seagrass in one place, creatures can take their time eating. The green sea turtle nibbles on the grasses for hours.

WHAT IS A SEAGRASS MEADOW?

UNDERWATER PLANT Seagrass is a plant that looks and feels like grass. It is the only plant that grows in salt water. It has roots, stems, and leaves, and it produces seeds.

MEADOWS Seagrass grows in shallow water near the shore. It spreads across large areas so that it looks like a field or meadow.

WARM AND COLD Most types of seagrass thrive in warm waters, but some are adapted to life in cold waters.

CLEANING Seagrass cleans the water and helps to keep the oceans healthy by releasing nutrients and oxygen.

What spotters need

It's best to swim rather than walk through seagrass so that you don't disturb the creatures that are hiding and feeding here. Use snorkeling gear to get a good look at this habitat.

SEAGRASS MEADOWS WATCH

Imagine swimming through a seagrass meadow. Many creatures come here to lay their eggs, so you might see their babies. They live here until they're big enough to swim out into open seas.

Camouflage

The bignose seagrass shrimp is as green as the seagrass. Creatures like this one find it easy to hide from predators in the meadow.

Bottom-feeders

Look out for the clean-up crew among the seagrass—sea cucumbers! They feed along the bottom and keep the meadow clean.

EYE SPOT HERMIT CRAB

Have you noticed a little creature peeking out of this shell? That's a hermit crab. This type of crab doesn't have a shell of its own, so it uses ones left behind by other creatures. This shell once belonged to a sea snail, and it makes the perfect home for the hermit crab— for now. When the hermit crab grows and the shell becomes too small, it will have to search for a new one.

WHERE IN THE WORLD?

LIVES: Mediterranean Sea

EATS: dead creatures

STATUS:
🌿 unknown

HOW BIG?

body up to
¾in (2cm) long

Hermit crabs are not true crabs, because they don't have their own shells.

The hermit crab needs a shell to protect its soft tail.

The walking legs are as long as the front claws.

There are two purple eye spots on the insides of its claws. These give this crab its name.

Eye spot hermit crab

IT'S WILD! If a hermit crab loses a leg or claw, it can grow another one.

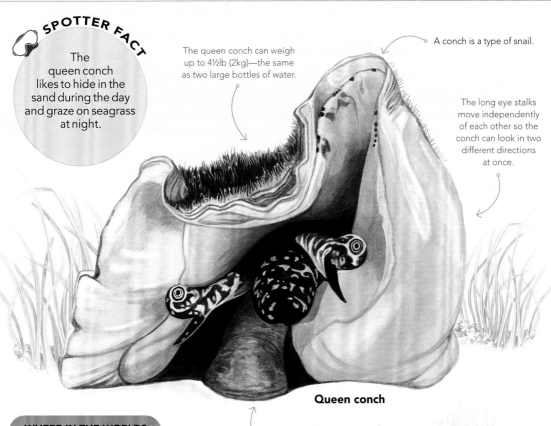

The queen conch can weigh up to 4½lb (2kg)—the same as two large bottles of water.

A conch is a type of snail.

The long eye stalks move independently of each other so the conch can look in two different directions at once.

Queen conch

The queen conch moves by pushing its foot against the ground. This lifts the shell and throws it forwards.

WHERE IN THE WORLD?

LIVES: Caribbean Sea and Atlantic Ocean around Bermuda

EATS: seagrass and algae

STATUS:
🐚 unknown

HOW BIG?

12in (30cm) long

QUEEN CONCH

Everything takes time with this strange-looking creature. The queen conch has to carry a heavy pink-and-orange swirly shell with it wherever it goes. This is why it moves at snail's pace over the seagrass. The queen conch also takes many years to grow and have babies. It's in no rush, because it can live as long as 30 years!

WHERE IN THE WORLD?

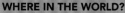

LIVES: waters around Australia

EATS: sea urchins, crustaceans, mollusks and small fish

STATUS:
🌿 least concern

HOW BIG?

30–37in (75–95cm) long

PORT JACKSON SHARK

You can easily recognize this shark by the black bands over its eyes and on its back. The Port Jackson shark only swims around at night when it's hungry. Keep an eye out for movement in the dark. During the day, you might see it resting in a cave or under a rock.

SPOTTER FACT

Each shark's head has a slightly different pattern. Scientists take photos of each one to identify them.

The black pattern on the gray body makes it difficult to spot the shark among shady seagrass.

This shark has a broad, flat head and a black crest above its eyes.

Port Jackson shark

The shark's flat teeth can crush crabs and other creatures with hard shells.

RED CUSHION SEA STAR

You'll have to look very carefully to spot a red cushion sea star in the seagrass. You might think a red creature would stand out, but it's only young sea stars that come to the meadow. These youngsters are green and blend perfectly with the grasses. Once the sea star gets bigger, it turns red and moves to sandy seabeds and coral reefs.

WHERE IN THE WORLD?

LIVES: Caribbean Sea and Atlantic Ocean

EATS: sea urchins, sponges, and algae

STATUS:
⬗ unknown

HOW BIG?

20in (50cm) wide

If another creatures bites off an arm, the sea star can grow it back.

Red cushion sea star

The sea star moves by using its tube feet on the underside.

IT'S WILD! After collecting its food, the sea star turns its belly inside out to eat it.

ATLANTIC HORSESHOE CRAB

WHERE IN THE WORLD?

LIVES: Atlantic coast of North America

EATS: marine worms, clams, snails, and algae

STATUS:
 vulnerable

HOW BIG?

females 19in (48cm) long; males 14in (36cm) long

If you come face to face with a horseshoe crab, you're looking at one of the world's oldest types of creature. Horseshoe crabs existed 450 million years ago—long before dinosaurs roamed Earth! Today's horseshoe crabs look very similar to their ancient relatives. Despite the name, they're not crabs, but part of the family of scorpions and spiders.

IN DANGER!

People catch horseshoe crabs to use as bait for conches and eels. This is now illegal in some places.

It has 10 eyes scattered around its body, with two large ones specifically for finding mates.

There are three parts to the body—a horseshoe-shaped head, a middle, and a long, pointy tail. The crab is heavily armored, like a tank.

Its blood contains copper, which makes it blue rather than the usual red.

Atlantic horseshoe crab

The horseshoe crab has six pairs of legs, but uses only five pairs for walking.

LONG-SNOUTED SEAHORSE

With its flexible tail, the seahorse can hold on to things like people can with their hands. You'll often see the seahorse curl its tail around the seagrass. It does this to stop itself being swept away by the current, because it's not very good at swimming.

DON'T MISS!

Look for tiny newborn seahorses. It's the fathers who give birth, keeping the eggs in their pouch until they're born.

The seahorse has no teeth. It just sucks up its favorite food with its long snout.

WHERE IN THE WORLD?

LIVES: eastern Atlantic Ocean and Mediterranean and Black seas

EATS: small crustaceans, fish eggs, and plankton

STATUS:
⬥ unknown

HOW BIG?

3–8in (8.5–21cm) long

The tail is curled up at the end when not in use.

This soft fin helps the seahorse to swim, but it isn't very strong.

Long-snouted seahorse

WEST INDIAN MANATEE

Seagrass is the manatee's favorite meal. When it finds a patch of seagrass on the ocean floor, it moves its lips around and plucks it off. A manatee is slow-moving, so it takes its time—you can watch this creature feeding for hours. The manatee's habit of grazing like a land animal is why it's also called a sea cow.

WHERE IN THE WORLD?

LIVES: Caribbean Sea and western Atlantic Ocean

EATS: seagrass and other plants

STATUS: vulnerable

HOW BIG?

8–13ft (2.5–4m) long

West Indian manatee

The skin is thick and wrinkled, with a few hairs.

The tail is the shape of a paddle.

IN DANGER!

Manatees can be hit by boats. Speed limits make speedboats drive more slowly to help sailors avoid them.

The two front flippers are for steering and holding on to plants.

A manatee can move each side of its thick lips separately.

IT'S WILD! A manatee can eat up to 10 percent of its body weight in a single day.

GREEN SEA TURTLE

Look who's come to the meadow to eat! The green sea turtle's sharp beak is perfect for munching on seagrass and scraping algae off rocks. This creature likes to return to the same spots for a tasty meal, so you'll be sure to see it again.

WHERE IN THE WORLD?

LIVES: Atlantic, Pacific, and Indian oceans, and Mediterranean Sea

EATS: seagrass and algae

STATUS: endangered

HOW BIG?

3–4ft (1–1.2m) long

The big front flippers act like paddles. The turtle is a fast swimmer.

The shell, called a carapace, is shaped like a teardrop. It covers almost all of the turtle's body, except for the head and four flippers.

The beak is like a sharp tool with jagged edges.

IN DANGER!
Turtles can be injured by litter and forgotten fishing nets. It's important to keep the oceans clean to protect them.

Green sea turtle

BIGNOSE SEAGRASS SHRIMP

This creature's name is a big clue for what you're looking for. The shrimp's body looks just like the green leaves of seagrass and is well hidden in the meadow. The *bignose* part of its name describes its head. It is long and pointy and looks like a big nose.

LIVES: Indian Ocean and Red Sea

EATS: plants

STATUS:
◢ unknown

HOW BIG?

up to 8in (20cm) long

The pointed head is called a rostrum. It helps the shrimp to stay steady in water and to protect itself from predators.

This shrimp has two bright white eyes that stand out on its green body.

The bignose shrimp uses its legs for swimming and for gripping onto seagrass.

Shrimp have a hard outer shell to protect their body, like a suit of armor.

SPOTTER FACT

Shrimp swim backward by bending their flexible tail and belly and wiggling their legs.

Bignose seagrass shrimp

ALLIGATOR PIPEFISH

When you have colors like this creature, it's easier to hide among the plants. The alligator pipefish comes in shades of green and yellow and looks just like the seagrass and algae around it. This makes it harder to spot—but as soon as it moves, you'll notice it. The alligator pipefish is a poor swimmer and likes to float in the ocean. It prefers to stay in calm, shallow waters.

WHERE IN THE WORLD?

LIVES: Indo-Pacific

EATS: zooplankton and other small creatures

STATUS:

 least concern

HOW BIG?

10–12in (26–30cm) long

Pipefish have a long, thin, snakelike body.

The pipefish's head is long and flat.

SPOTTER FACT

Just like its seahorse relative, the alligator pipefish wraps its tail around leaves to anchor itself.

Alligator pipefish

The body is covered with hard plates that help to protect the pipefish from predators.

The pipefish is related to the seahorse. They are both fish with long snouts that can't swim very well.

IT'S WILD! Male pipefish look after the female's eggs in a special pouch under their tail.

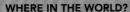

WHERE IN THE WORLD?

LIVES: southern Australian waters

EATS: algae and seagrass

STATUS:
🍃 vulnerable

HOW BIG?

shell 9in (23cm) long

GREENLIP ABALONE

An abalone is a type of sea snail. This one lives in the seagrass meadows of Australia. Here it grazes slowly on the green plants. You can recognize the greenlip abalone by looking at its foot—the large muscle inside the shell. It's green along the lip, or edge.

The oval abalone shell is very strong. It comes in shades of green and pink.

Greenlip abalone

The foot takes up most of the space inside the shell.

The abalone clings to rocks using this powerful foot. It is hard for predators such as Port Jackson sharks to pry it off.

DON'T MISS!
Look carefully. The abalone's shell is often covered with algae or small creatures, so it is well camouflaged.

CURLED OCTOPUS

You can probably guess why the curled octopus got its name—it curls up its eight arms when resting. To see it, you have to be patient. This octopus spends most of the day hiding between rocks and in crevices. When it's hungry, it will come out and move through the seagrass in search of crabs, shrimp, and other tasty things to eat.

WHERE IN THE WORLD?

LIVES: northeastern Atlantic Ocean and Mediterranean Sea

EATS: shrimp, lobsters, crabs, and fish

STATUS:
least concern

HOW BIG?

20in (50cm) long

This octopus is usually reddish-brown with a white underside. It can quickly change color to match its surroundings.

SPOTTER FACT

When threatened, the curled octopus releases dark ink to confuse predators. This gives it time to escape.

Its skin is covered in tiny bumps and some larger warts.

Curled octopus

The arms are slim and quite short, with a single row of suckers.

SNOWFLAKE MORAY EEL

Most moray eels live in coral reefs, but the snowflake moray eel also likes to explore seagrass meadows. Keep a careful watch. When a moray eel is hungry, it will bravely come out from its rocky hideaway and slip easily through the seagrass in search of food.

Moray eels have two sets of jaws—one for grabbing and one for swallowing food.

Snowflake moray eel

WHERE IN THE WORLD?

LIVES: Indo-Pacific

EATS: algae, plankton, and bits of waste

STATUS:
🍃 unknown

HOW BIG?

6½ft (2m) long

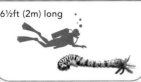

SNAKE SEA CUCUMBER

This creature has a very important job—to keep the ocean floor clean for other creatures. The snake sea cucumber sucks up algae and bits of waste with its tentacles. Without it, the algae would get out of control and overgrow the seagrass.

DON'T MISS!

Keep a lookout on the beach. This moray eel can leave the water and grab prey on land.

The eel moves through the water by wiggling its body like a wave.

The snowflake moray eel has a white body with two rows of black blotches. Its white areas look a bit like snowflakes.

WHERE IN THE WORLD?

LIVES: Indian and Pacific oceans

EATS: crab, shrimp, and small fish

STATUS: least concern

HOW BIG?

20in (50cm) long

This sea cucumber is often mistaken for a sea snake. Its body is only a couple of inches wide, but is very long.

The sea cucumber's body is covered in white and black speckled bands. It's also known as the spotted worm sea cucumber.

Snake sea cucumber

There are 15 tentacles around the mouth. These are for feeding.

IT'S WILD! There are more than 1,200 types of sea cucumber. The snake sea cucumber is the longest.

HOW TO SPOT IN OPEN SEAS

Away from land, the ocean stretches as far as the eye can see. In such a huge area, it can be hard to find smaller creatures like the blue sea dragon and the egg-yolk jellyfish. Keep a careful watch to spot a lone great white shark or a yellowfin tuna as it powers through the water, hunting for food.

WHAT ARE OPEN SEAS?

NO LAND IN SIGHT As the land disappears from view, you enter open seas. Scientists call this the pelagic zone.

CLEAR AND BLUE The water here is clean and clear. It appears bluer than the waters around the coast.

THE OCEAN SURFACE Nearly all ocean creatures live near the surface down to about 660ft (200 m).

MOVING AROUND Open seas give creatures almost endless space to live in. Some travel great distances.

Look out for the back fin
When fish swim at the surface of the water, their fins stick out. If the back fin is more than 3ft (1m) tall, it might be a great white shark.

Study the tail
Dolphins swim by moving their tail up and down, while sharks move theirs from side to side.

Great white shark

Be on the lookout
Picture yourself on a boat, with the vast ocean all around. Your best chance of spotting creatures in the open seas is when they break through the surface of the water.

Watch the swimming
Many fish have large, winglike fins on either side of their body. These help them to change direction in the water.

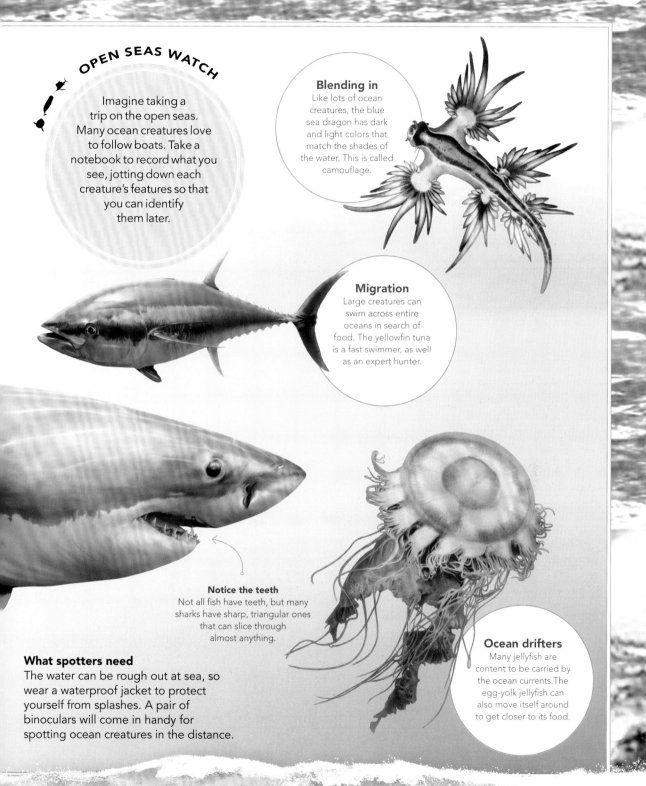

OPEN SEAS WATCH

Imagine taking a trip on the open seas. Many ocean creatures love to follow boats. Take a notebook to record what you see, jotting down each creature's features so that you can identify them later.

Blending in
Like lots of ocean creatures, the blue sea dragon has dark and light colors that match the shades of the water. This is called camouflage.

Migration
Large creatures can swim across entire oceans in search of food. The yellowfin tuna is a fast swimmer, as well as an expert hunter.

Notice the teeth
Not all fish have teeth, but many sharks have sharp, triangular ones that can slice through almost anything.

What spotters need
The water can be rough out at sea, so wear a waterproof jacket to protect yourself from splashes. A pair of binoculars will come in handy for spotting ocean creatures in the distance.

Ocean drifters
Many jellyfish are content to be carried by the ocean currents. The egg-yolk jellyfish can also move itself around to get closer to its food.

WHERE IN THE WORLD?

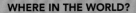
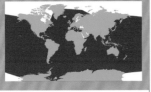

LIVES: all oceans, mainly in deep waters

EATS: squid, sharks, skates, and fish

STATUS:
🐟 vulnerable

HOW BIG?

36–60ft (11–18m) long

SPERM WHALE

Listen carefully if you're diving underwater and you might hear clicking sounds. A sperm whale uses these clicks to check what other ocean creatures are around. Notice how the sounds get faster, now sounding like a squeaky door. This means the whale has found food nearby. It might be a squid, its favorite meal.

This whale is one of the ocean's deepest divers. It can go down to 7,200ft (2,200m).

ATLANTIC BLUEFIN TUNA

WHERE IN THE WORLD?

LIVES: North Atlantic Ocean and Mediterranean Sea

EATS: small fish, squid, crabs, shrimp, and zooplankton

STATUS:
🐟 least concern

HOW BIG?

6½ft (2m) long

With its strong, perfectly shaped tail, this huge tuna speeds through the water. You might catch a glimpse of metallic blue and recognize it by its beautiful colors.

The tuna can pull back its top and side fins to go faster in the water.

Atlantic bluefin tuna

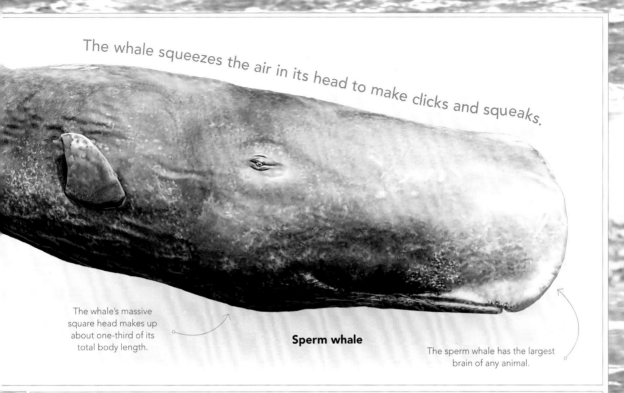

The whale squeezes the air in its head to make clicks and squeaks.

The whale's massive square head makes up about one-third of its total body length.

Sperm whale

The sperm whale has the largest brain of any animal.

YELLOWFIN TUNA

Watch out! This superfast fish will whoosh past you in an instant, but you may just see a flash of its yellow fins. This is what gives this tuna its name.

WHERE IN THE WORLD?

LIVES: warm waters

EATS: small fish, squids, crabs, shrimp, and zooplankton

STATUS:
 least concern

HOW BIG?

5ft (1.5m) long

Yellowfin tuna

Tuna are great travelers. They can swim across an entire ocean.

PELAGIC THRESHER

Fish often crowd together in a ball to make it more difficult for hungry predators to eat them. The thresher has a secret weapon against this— its long, powerful tail. Watch closely as the shark swims toward the closely packed ball of fish, then stops and whips its tail over its head. WHACK! The fish are stunned by the tail slap and are now easy for the shark to catch.

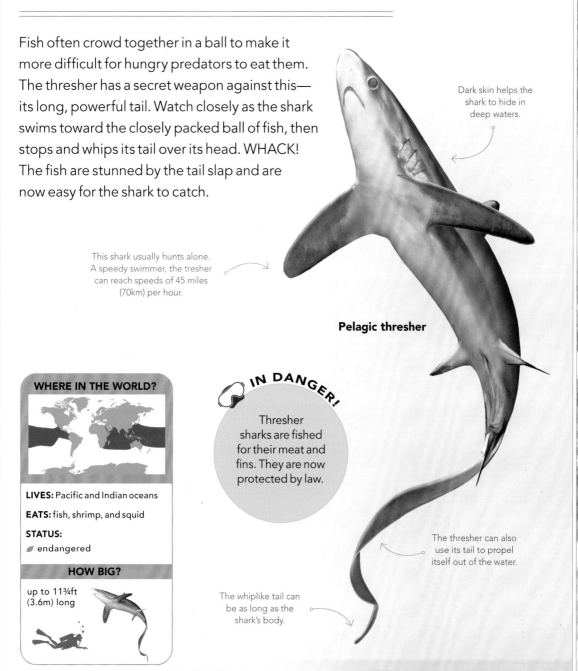

Dark skin helps the shark to hide in deep waters.

This shark usually hunts alone. A speedy swimmer, the tresher can reach speeds of 45 miles (70km) per hour.

Pelagic thresher

IN DANGER!

Thresher sharks are fished for their meat and fins. They are now protected by law.

The thresher can also use its tail to propel itself out of the water.

The whiplike tail can be as long as the shark's body.

WHERE IN THE WORLD?

LIVES: Pacific and Indian oceans

EATS: fish, shrimp, and squid

STATUS:
endangered

HOW BIG?

up to 11¾ft (3.6m) long

EGG-YOLK JELLYFISH

LIVES: Pacific, Atlantic, and western Indian oceans, and Mediterranean Sea

EATS: other jellyfish

STATUS:
🍃 unknown

HOW BIG?

bell up to 24in (60cm) wide; tentacles up to 20ft (6m) long

There are many strange creatures in the ocean, but you probably didn't expect to see one that looks like an uncooked egg! The egg-yolk jellyfish's name comes from its milky-white bell and the yellow part at its center. See how strong currents can change the shape of its soft, delicate body so that it can also look like a fried egg with a broken yolk.

Jellyfish usually just drift with the currents, but this one sometimes pulses its bell to move around.

The jellyfish waits for other creatures to come close and get tangled up in its tentacles. Then it grabs them with its feeding arms.

Egg-yolk jellyfish

DON'T MISS!

Look out for the jellyfish's passengers. Baby crabs and other crustaceans hitch a ride inside and on top of its bell.

Long, see-through tentacles trail behind the jellyfish. They are covered with stinging cells to paralyze its prey.

WHERE IN THE WORLD?

LIVES: warm and cool waters

EATS: fish, squid, dolphins, and other sharks

STATUS:
endangered

HOW BIG?

9ft (2.7m) long

SHORTFIN MAKO

The shortfin mako, with its slender body, speedily patrols the water for prey. Not even tuna and other fast-swimming fish are safe from it.

The mako is the fastest of all sharks. Its top speed is 46mph (74kmph).

Shortfin mako

WHERE IN THE WORLD?

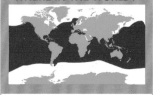

LIVES: warm and cool waters

EATS: fish, squid, crustaceans, and sometimes seabirds and dead whales

STATUS:
near threatened

HOW BIG?

10¾ft (3.3m) long

BLUE SHARK

You might recognize this shark from its huge black eyes and long, pointed snout. You'll often see it alone, but blue sharks sometimes swim together in all-female or all-male groups.

The metallic-blue skin is what gives this shark its name.

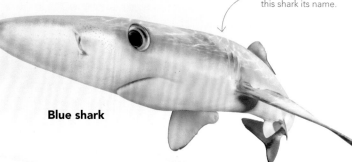

Blue shark

OCEANIC SUNFISH

You're most likely to spot this oddly shaped fish when it floats sideways near the surface. It seems to be sunbathing, which is why it's called a sunfish. Scientists think it's warming itself up after swimming in cooler water. You might also see it sucking up jellyfish, its favorite food.

WHERE IN THE WORLD?

LIVES: warm and cool waters

EATS: jellyfish, zooplankton, small fish, and crustaceans

STATUS:
vulnerable

HOW BIG?

up to 10¾ft (3.3.m) long

The tail fin folds over on itself as it grows. Without a proper tail, the sunfish looks like a giant swimming head.

Oceanic sunfish

This the world's heaviest bony fish, weighing up to 6,000lb (2,800kg).

Its teeth are joined together to create a beaklike mouth.

IN DANGER!
Sunfish struggle to breathe when they are caught in large fishing nets. They may also eat plastic by mistake.

The sunfish is flat and circular. It is often taller than it is long.

BLUE SEA DRAGON

The little blue sea dragon swims belly side up when it's on the surface, for one very good reason. The sea slug's blue-and-white belly stripes mean it blends perfectly with the ocean. It goes unnoticed by passing birds, but what about you?

Scientists believe the blue colors protects the slug from the sun's rays.

To keep itself afloat on the surface, the blue sea dragon swallows a tiny air bubble.

Like most sea slugs, the blue sea dragon has both male and female parts.

The blue sea dragon is known by many names. The shape of its body gives it one of them—the blue angel.

The blue sea dragon has a powerful sting.

Blue sea dragon

WHERE IN THE WORLD?

LIVES: warm waters

EATS: jellyfish

STATUS:
unknown

HOW BIG?

up to 1½in (4cm) long

SPOTTER FACT

The blue sea dragon is a very rare sight in the open ocean. You're most likely to spot it washed up on beaches.

COWNOSE RAY

Dive into a special kind of parade! Thousands of cownose rays are swimming near the surface as they travel from one part of the ocean to another. Together, they are safe from the sharks that want to eat them. After their long journey, the rays stay close to the coast.

WHERE IN THE WORLD?

LIVES: western Atlantic Ocean

EATS: clams, crabs, lobsters, and snails

STATUS:
🍃 vulnerable

HOW BIG?

4ft (1.2m) wide

The cownose ray glides through the water with these pointed pectoral fins.

IN DANGER!
This ray grows slowly and has only a few pups. If too many are caught, there aren't enough to mate with each other.

The largest cownose rays have a wingspan of 7ft (2.1m).

Cownose ray

This ray's forehead looks like the nose of a cow.

PORTUGUESE MAN-OF-WAR

A balloonlike float on the surface of the water can mean only one thing—it's a Portuguese man-of-war. It uses its float as a sail to catch the wind and move across the open seas. This ocean drifter is named after an old-fashioned Portuguese warship that had large sails.

WHERE IN THE WORLD?

LIVES: warm waters

EATS: small fish, crustaceans, and plankton

STATUS:
▰ unknown

HOW BIG?

float 12in (30cm) long and 5in (12cm) wide; tentacles 33–100ft (10–30m) long

The float, or bladder, is filled with gas. This makes it float on the water.

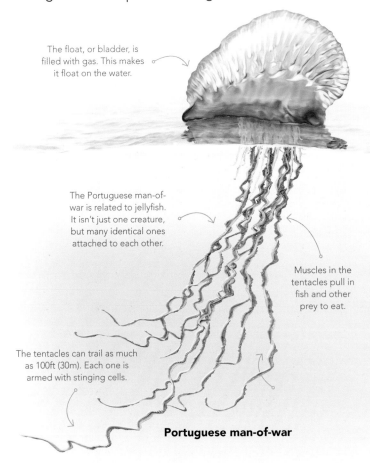

The Portuguese man-of-war is related to jellyfish. It isn't just one creature, but many identical ones attached to each other.

Muscles in the tentacles pull in fish and other prey to eat.

The tentacles can trail as much as 100ft (30m). Each one is armed with stinging cells.

Portuguese man-of-war

Man-of-war fish
The man-of-war fish lives between the Portuguese man-of-war's tentacles. It swims cleverly between them to avoid being stung.

IT'S WILD! Sometimes more than 1,000 Portuguese man-of-wars drift alongside each other.

FLYING FISH

If you spot something flying through the air that looks like a fish, you're not seeing things! This fish jumps out of the water and glides through the air to escape from predators.

LIVES: Atlantic Ocean and Caribbean Sea

EATS: plankton

STATUS:
least concern

HOW BIG?

up to 18in (45cm) long

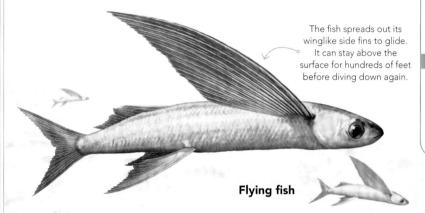

The fish spreads out its winglike side fins to glide. It can stay above the surface for hundreds of feet before diving down again.

Flying fish

ATLANTIC SAILFISH

Meet the fastest fish of all—the sailfish. It can swim more speedily than the fastest land animal, the cheetah, can run. This fish is named after the large fin on its back, which looks like a sail.

WHERE IN THE WORLD?

LIVES: Atlantic Ocean and Caribbean and Mediterranean seas

EATS: fish, crustaceans, squid, and octopus

STATUS:
unknown

HOW BIG?

8ft (2.4m) long

The sailfish uses its long, pointy bill to slash at groups of fish. This makes them easier to catch.

Atlantic sailfish

GREAT WHITE SHARK

WHERE IN THE WORLD?

LIVES: all ocean, except for cold waters of Southern and Arctic oceans

EATS: fish, sea turtles, other sharks, seabirds, seals, and other marine mammals

STATUS:
vulnerable

HOW BIG?

up to 21ft (6.4m) long

The ocean's biggest predatory fish is known as the king of the ocean. Armed with a massive jaw and razor-sharp teeth, the great white shark is an amazing hunter. It can easily tackle large prey, such as seals and even other sharks. The great white shark roams huge distances throughout its long life. It prefers deep water, so it is rare to spot one.

When the shark swims in shallow water, the back fin sometimes pokes up above the surface.

DON'T MISS!
Head to a coast or river mouth if you want to spot shark pups. They are more than 3ft (1m) long.

The powerful tail fin helps it speed through the water at 35 miles (50km) per hour.

Great white shark

This shark lives for about 70 years.

The great white shark gets its name from its huge size and white belly.

SALMON SHARK

Salmon sharks can swim through the vast oceans with ease. They feel comfortable in cold water because, unusually for a fish, they are able to keep their bodies warm. They swim great distances through the ocean, searching for their favorite food—salmon.

WHERE IN THE WORLD?

LIVES: North Pacific Ocean

EATS: mainly salmon

STATUS:
🌿 least concern

HOW BIG?

6½–9ft (2–3m) long

With its short, cone-shaped snout, the salmon shark is often mistaken for a great white shark.

The salmon shark is named for its love of salmon.

There are many dark blotches on its white belly.

SPOTTER FACT

The salmon shark's bladelike teeth are similar to those of the great white shark, but smaller.

The salmon shark lives for at least 25 years.

Salmon shark

LEATHERBACK TURTLE

Meet one of the world's most impressive long-distance travelers. After two adventurous years roaming the oceans, this huge leatherback turtle is on a mission. She is ready to lay her eggs. To do so, she makes the long journey back to the exact same beach where she was born and took her first swim.

Leatherback turtle

The leatherback is the largest turtle in the world. It has existed since the time of the dinosaurs.

Turtle hatchlings
After the mother leatherback has dug a deep pit and laid her eggs, she returns to the ocean. Two months later, her babies hatch, climb out of the nest, and race toward the water. They now have to fend for themselves.

IN DANGER!
Leatherbacks get tangled in fishing nets and lines. They also swallow plastic bags, which they mistake for jellyfish.

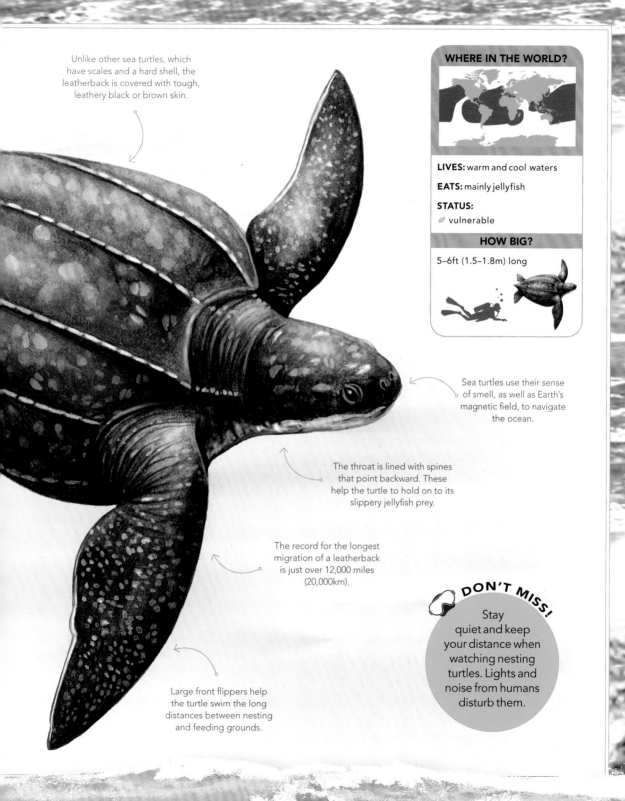

Unlike other sea turtles, which have scales and a hard shell, the leatherback is covered with tough, leathery black or brown skin.

WHERE IN THE WORLD?

LIVES: warm and cool waters

EATS: mainly jellyfish

STATUS:
vulnerable

HOW BIG?

5–6ft (1.5–1.8m) long

Sea turtles use their sense of smell, as well as Earth's magnetic field, to navigate the ocean.

The throat is lined with spines that point backward. These help the turtle to hold on to its slippery jellyfish prey.

The record for the longest migration of a leatherback is just over 12,000 miles (20,000km).

DON'T MISS!
Stay quiet and keep your distance when watching nesting turtles. Lights and noise from humans disturb them.

Large front flippers help the turtle swim the long distances between nesting and feeding grounds.

GIANT MANTA RAY

A giant manta ray glides gracefully through the water right in front of you. Are you wondering where it will go next? This intelligent creature travels all over the world. It finds it way by using landmarks in the ocean, such as underwater mountains.

WHERE IN THE WORLD?

LIVES: warm and cool waters

EATS: plankton

STATUS:
🍃 endangered

HOW BIG?

23ft (7m) wide

The giant manta is the largest type of ray.

The manta extends these two head parts to channel water into its mouth. The mouth filters plankton from the water.

The fins on either side look like wings when the manta swims.

Giant manta ray

A female manta gives birth to a pup only every four or five years.

IN DANGER!

Some people fish for manta rays on purpose. They are easy to catch because they swim very slowly.

WHERE IN THE WORLD?

LIVES: Indian Ocean and warm waters of Pacific and Atlantic oceans

EATS: fish, octopus, and shrimp

STATUS:
🍃 least concern

HOW BIG?

4½ft (1.4m) long

GREAT BARRACUDA

There are more than 20 species of barracuda, but this one is the best known. You can recognize the great barracuda by its large size, shiny silver body, and sharp teeth. Watch out for its quick moves—this hunter strikes as soon as it spots a meal.

The great barracuda has a head that is almost flat at the top.

There are about 20 dark bars on the sides of its deep, silvery body.

Great barracuda

The large mouth is full of sharp, pointy teeth.

DON'T MISS!

In the open ocean, this fish likes to stay near the surface by itself. It waits to ambush passing prey.

IT'S WILD! The barracuda usually prefers to be alone, but sometimes you can spot it in small groups.

BLUE WHALE

Picture a colossal creature that's as big as two buses! At around 100ft (30m) long, the blue whale is the largest animal that has ever existed. This shy and gentle giant is a rare sight. You might hear it before you see it, because it's not just the biggest creature on the planet—it's also one of the loudest. Scientists think its calls can be heard by other whales up to 1,000 miles (1,600km) away.

WHERE IN THE WORLD?

LIVES: all oceans except Arctic

EATS: krill

STATUS: endangered

HOW BIG?

up to 110ft (33m) long

The blowhole on top of its head is where the whale breathes air.

The whale opens its huge mouth to gulp lots of water. It has special filters called baleens to trap krill and allow the water to escape.

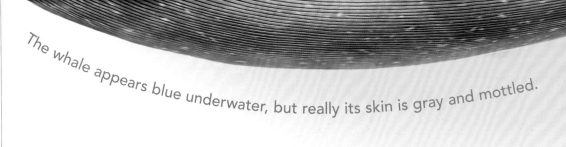

The whale appears blue underwater, but really its skin is gray and mottled.

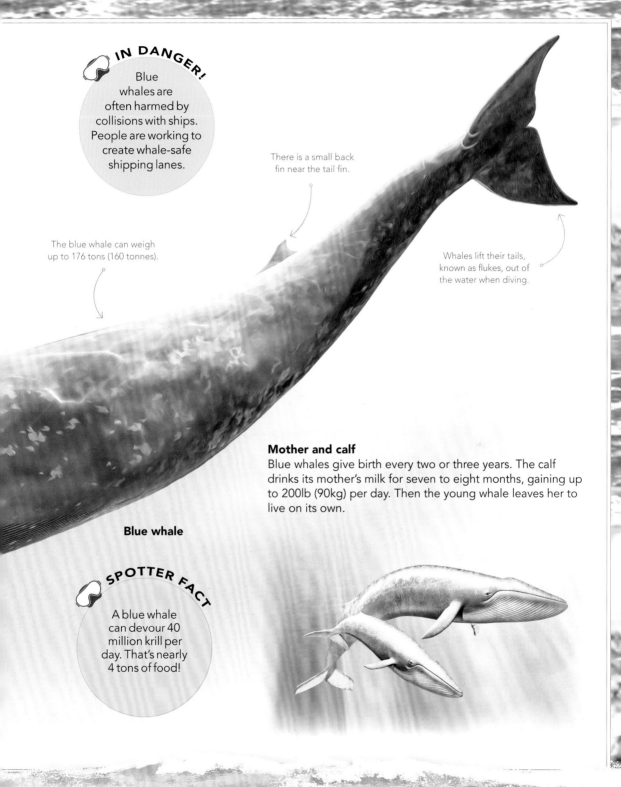

IN DANGER!
Blue whales are often harmed by collisions with ships. People are working to create whale-safe shipping lanes.

There is a small back fin near the tail fin.

The blue whale can weigh up to 176 tons (160 tonnes).

Whales lift their tails, known as flukes, out of the water when diving.

Mother and calf
Blue whales give birth every two or three years. The calf drinks its mother's milk for seven to eight months, gaining up to 200lb (90kg) per day. Then the young whale leaves her to live on its own.

Blue whale

SPOTTER FACT
A blue whale can devour 40 million krill per day. That's nearly 4 tons of food!

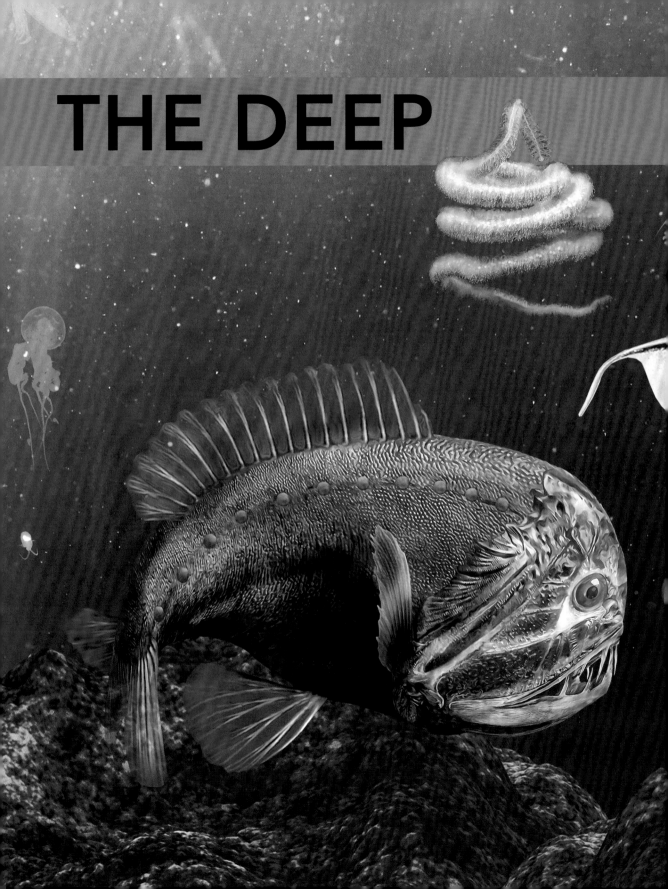

THE DEEP

HOW TO SPOT IN THE DEEP

Imagine what it's like to go down to the deepest parts of the ocean. Sunlight can't reach this far and creatures like the pink see-through fantasia and bloodybelly comb jelly suddenly loom out of the dark. In the inky blackness, you'll also see flickering lights from creatures such as the humpback anglerfish.

Study the tentacles
This far down, there's not much to eat other than marine snow. Many creatures have tentacles to push food into their mouths.

Expect the unexpected
Very little of the deep ocean has been explored. Be prepared to spot some strange and rarely seen ocean creatures.

DEEP-SEA WATCH

Imagine seeing billions of creatures swim from the deep ocean to the surface every night, mainly to find food. It's the biggest migration of animals on the planet! Research the creatures you expect to see.

Pink see-through fantasia

Notice behaviour
Sea cucumbers crawl around on the seabed. If you see one lifting off and swimming, it must be the pink see-through fantasia.

Look inside
Many creatures in the deep are transparent so they can't be easily spotted by predators. You can see the organs inside the pink see-through fantasia.

WHAT IS THE DEEP OCEAN?

650ft (200m) There is very little sunlight. Many creatures living here and below are bioluminescent—they make their own light.

3,300ft (1,000m) At this depth, there is no sunlight at all. No plants live here and most creatures survive on tiny bits called marine snow marine snow or by preying on other creatures.

13,000ft (4,000m) The water is near freezing. Very few creatures can survive the extreme pressure of having so much water above them.

20,000ft (6,000m) This part of the ocean mostly consists of long and narrow valleys called trenches.

36,000ft (11,000m) This is the deepest part of the ocean. The water feels very heavy—like 100 elephants on your head.

What spotters need

No human has ever dived below 1,089ft (332m), so you have to be in a submarine to go any deeper. Most explorers of the very deep ocean use a vehicle that has no people in it. It is steered from a boat on the surface and sends back images for spotters to see.

Making light

Creatures make their own light to attract prey or a mate in the dark. The humpback anglerfish has a glowing lure that brings prey toward its huge mouth.

Colored red

In the deep ocean, the color red looks black. Creatures that are red, like the bloodybelly comb jelly, are almost impossible for predators to see.

Soft bodies

Most deep-sea creatures, such as the balloon worm, have soft, watery bodies. This helps them cope with the pressure of the water above them.

LIVES: warm and cool waters; 250–16,400ft (75–5,000m) deep

EATS: (young) zooplankton; (adults) fish, squid, and crustaceans

STATUS:
◢ least concern

HOW BIG?

up to 7in (18cm) long

COMMON FANGTOOTH

Don't be afraid when you meet this scary-looking fish with its long, sharp teeth. The common fangtooth is quite small and won't harm you. It searches the ocean from top to bottom until it comes across fish to eat. Then it uses its longest teeth, or fangs, like a cage to trap them.

The teeth slot into special pockets so that the fish doesn't pierce its own brain when it closes its mouth.

There are 17–20 soft rays, or bones, in the fangtooth's back fin.

The fangtooth's brownish-black body helps it hide in the dark waters.

SPOTTER FACT

The fangtooth can sense the chemicals that other fish give off. This helps it to find food in the dark.

Common fangtooth

TRIPOD FISH

Can you make out a fish that looks like it's standing on stilts? It's the tripod fish, waiting patiently for a meal to come by.

The tail fin helps the fish to keep steady when it's standing on the seabed.

Tripod fish

These fins are stiff when the fish stands. They become soft when it swims.

WHERE IN THE WORLD?

LIVES: Atlantic, Indian, and Pacific oceans; 3,000–15,500ft (900–4,700m) deep

EATS: plankton and other small creatures

STATUS:
least concern

HOW BIG?

12in (30cm) long

WOOLLY SIPHONOPHORE

WHERE IN THE WORLD?

LIVES: North Pacific Ocean; 2,000–6,000ft (600–1,800m) deep

EATS: plankton, small fish, and crustaceans

STATUS:
unknown

HOW BIG?

usually 6½ft (2m) long, but can be 16ft (5m) or more

That long, fluffy creature you see drifting through the ocean is made up of thousands of tiny creatures living together as a group, or colony.

Siphonophores float in the ocean current.

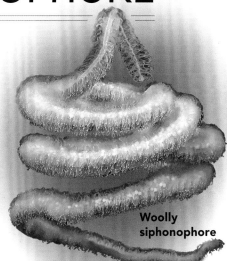

Woolly siphonophore

SHINING BOMBER WORM

WHERE IN THE WORLD?

LIVES: northeastern Pacific Ocean; 8,900–11,800ft (2,700–3,600m) deep

EATS: unknown

STATUS: unknown

HOW BIG?

1in (3cm) long

You might see glowing green balls before you spot the tiny shining bomber worm. The worm releases the "bombs" to confuse predators.

Shining bomber worm

Sharp bristles work like paddles so that the worm can move about.

PYGMY SHARK

When you look at this little shark from above, it's just black and brown. If you look from underneath, you'll see it glows blue to disguise its shape from predators lurking below.

WHERE IN THE WORLD?

LIVES: warm and cool waters; up to 6,000ft (1,800m) deep

EATS: squid, fish, and crustaceans

STATUS: least concern

HOW BIG?

up to 12in (30cm) long

The pygmy shark follows squid and fish to the surface at night.

Pygmy shark

GIANT SQUID

Look out—you're staring into an eye that's bigger than a football! It belongs to the giant squid. Only one other creature in the animal kingdom, the colossal squid, has eyes this large.

WHERE IN THE WORLD?

LIVES: all oceans; 650–3,000ft (200–900m) deep

EATS: crustaceans, fish, and other squids

STATUS:
🍃 least concern

HOW BIG?

up to 43ft (13m) long

The giant squid's eyes measure 10½in (27cm) across. Their size means the squid can spot predators from a distance.

The main part of the squid's body is called the mantle. The longest mantle on record is 7¼ft (2.25m).

The squid has two long tentacles. These grab prey and bring them up to the squid's beaklike mouth.

Giant squid

The ends of the tentacles are covered with strong suckers.

SPOTTER FACT

It's rare to find a giant squid in the ocean. Scientists usually study them when they wash ashore.

VAMPIRE SQUID

This creature isn't really a squid. It's just called a squid because it has eight arms, like squids do. The vampire squid's arms are connected by thick skin. This makes it look like it's wearing a dark cape, like a vampire. There are lights on the end of the arms that can be flashed to scare off predators.

WHERE IN THE WORLD?

LIVES: warm and cool waters; 2,000–4,000ft (600–1,200m) deep

EATS: zooplankton and marine snow

STATUS: unknown

HOW BIG?

12in (30cm) long

The fins on the squid's sides are for swimming and steering.

The vampire squid closes its webbed arms around food. The arms then push the food into its mouth.

Vampire squid

If it's startled, the vampire squid wraps its arms around its body, turning the "cape" inside out. This helps it to stay safe from hungry predators.

SPOTTER FACT

The vampire squid is the only creature of its kind. This species has existed for millions of years.

WHERE IN THE WORLD?

LIVES: Indian, Atlantic, and Pacific oceans; up to 4,900ft (1,500m) deep

EATS: fish and squid

STATUS:
least concern

HOW BIG?

up to 6ft (2m) long

FRILLED SHARK

Not many people have ever seen a frilled shark, but maybe you'll be lucky. This awesome predator has 300 hooked teeth arranged in 25 rows.

A frilled shark can be pregnant for over three years.

The back fins are much larger than those on the front.

Frilled shark

BALLOON WORM

It's hard to believe this little balloonlike creature is a worm. Keep your eyes peeled. It's almost transparent and hard to spot in the water.

WHERE IN THE WORLD?

LIVES: Pacific Ocean; 650–7,200ft (200–2,200m) deep

EATS: marine snow

STATUS:
unknown

HOW BIG?

1–1½in (2.5–4cm) long

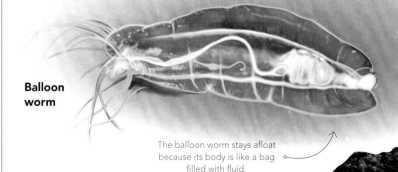

Balloon worm

The balloon worm stays afloat because its body is like a bag filled with fluid.

MARIANA SNAILFISH

You'll need to be in a submarine to find one of the world's deepest-living fish—the Mariana snailfish. It lives in the Mariana Trench, which is the deepest place on Earth.

It's called a snailfish because its body is covered in slime, like a land snail.

Mariana snailfish

WHERE IN THE WORLD?

LIVES: Mariana Trench in western Pacific Ocean; 26,000ft (8,000m) deep

EATS: crustaceans

STATUS:
🍂 unknown

HOW BIG?

up to 11in (29cm) long

BIGFIN SQUID

WHERE IN THE WORLD?

LIVES: Pacific and Atlantic oceans; up to 20,000ft (6,200m) deep

EATS: probably crustaceans and fish

STATUS:
🍂 unknown

HOW BIG?

at least 20ft (6m) long

You might become one of the lucky few to see the rare bigfin squid. It's named after its large fins, which are almost as long as its body.

The bigfin squid has eight arms and two tentacles. Unusually for a squid, these are all the same length.

Bigfin squid

STRAWBERRY SQUID

Look, this squid has two different eyes! One eye is big and yellowy-green. It looks up in the dim light to see shadows of prey passing by. The smaller blue eye can see the flashes of light given off by other creatures in the dark water below.

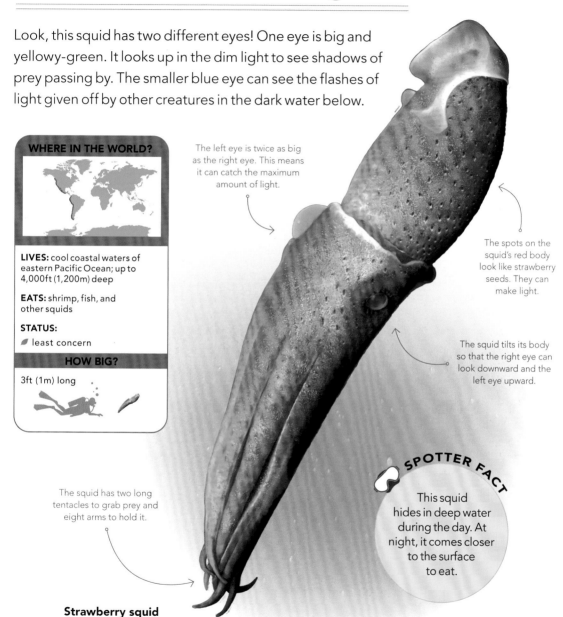

WHERE IN THE WORLD?

LIVES: cool coastal waters of eastern Pacific Ocean; up to 4,000ft (1,200m) deep

EATS: shrimp, fish, and other squids

STATUS:
least concern

HOW BIG?

3ft (1m) long

The left eye is twice as big as the right eye. This means it can catch the maximum amount of light.

The spots on the squid's red body look like strawberry seeds. They can make light.

The squid tilts its body so that the right eye can look downward and the left eye upward.

The squid has two long tentacles to grab prey and eight arms to hold it.

Strawberry squid

SPOTTER FACT

This squid hides in deep water during the day. At night, it comes closer to the surface to eat.

IT'S WILD! The lights on the strawberry squid's body help it to hide its shape from predators.

This creature is sometimes called the headless chicken monster because it looks like a chicken that doesn't have a head.

Tube-shaped tentacles are used to eat things from the ocean floor.

See-through skin means you can see all its internal organs.

Pink see-through fantasia

SPOTTER FACT

The fantasia's color depends on its size. Small ones are pink and larger ones are brownish-red or purple.

The fantasia's jellylike body can produce light to distract predators.

PINK SEE-THROUGH FANTASIA

Have you ever heard of a swimming cucumber? Most types of sea cucumber can't swim, but the pink see-through fantasia can lift off the seabed and move to other parts of the ocean using its two fins. This way, it can escape from predators or explore new areas for food.

WHERE IN THE WORLD?

LIVES: all oceans; 18,700ft (5,700m) deep

EATS: sediment

STATUS:
🐟 unknown

HOW BIG?

up to 10in (25cm) long

DEEP-SEA BRITTLE STAR

The brittle star is related to the sea star, but you'll see that it's quite different. This creature has a small, disk-shaped body instead of a wide one. Its five arms are very long and thin rather than thick and spongy.

WHERE IN THE WORLD?

LIVES: Gulf of Mexico; up to 21,300ft (6,500m) deep

EATS: small creatures, such as crustaceans and zooplankton

STATUS:
✒ unknown

HOW BIG?

up to 8in (20cm) wide, including arms

Brittle stars wrap themselves around deep-sea corals. They grab tiny bits of food floating past in the water.

DON'T MISS!

Look out for brittle stars on the move. They wiggle their arms to walk and flick them around to swim.

If attacked, the brittle star can drop an arm to escape. The arm will regrow later.

Deep-sea brittle star

HUMPBACK ANGLERFISH

The female anglerfish is a cunning hunter. Do you see that glowing lure in the pitch-black water? That's a trick. When she wiggles her lure, other fish think it's something to eat. As soon as they come close, she gobbles them up!

WHERE IN THE WORLD?

LIVES: warm and cool waters; up to 8,900ft (2,700m) deep

EATS: small fish and crustaceans

STATUS:
🍃 least concern

HOW BIG?

females 6in (15cm) long; males 1¼in (3cm) long

All anglerfish have short fins on their backs. Female humpback anglerfish have short, rounded bodies.

Humpback anglerfish

The lure is filled with bacteria that make their own light. Only the female anglerfish has a lure.

SPOTTER FACT
There are more than 200 types of anglerfish. Some live in very deep and cold waters and others in warm shallows.

Anglerfish have big mouths filled with lots of sharp, see-through teeth. They can swallow prey that are twice as big as they are.

GULPER EEL

The first thing you'll notice about this eel is its huge mouth. It makes up a large part of the eel's body and can stretch out wide to gulp down fish whole.

Gulper eel

Deep black skin means the eel is barely visible in the dark.

The huge lower jaw looks like the pouch of a pelican. That's why it's also called the pelican eel.

WHERE IN THE WORLD?

LIVES: warm and cool waters; 9,000ft (3,000m) deep

EATS: fish, crustaceans, and squid

STATUS:
least concern

HOW BIG?

3ft (1m) long

GIANT DEEP-SEA NUDIBRANCH

The round creature you see crawling slowly across the ocean floor is a type of snail. It can't see very well, so feels and smells to find its way.

The feeding tentacles are at the front.

Giant deep-sea nudibranch

WHERE IN THE WORLD?

LIVES: northeastern Pacific Ocean; 10,800ft (3,300m) deep

EATS: unknown

STATUS:
unknown

HOW BIG?

12in (30cm) long

BARRELEYE

Peek inside this fish's see-through head to see its bright green, barrel-shaped eyes. The barreleye can see both above and in front of its head.

WHERE IN THE WORLD?

LIVES: North Pacific Ocean; up to 4,000ft (1,200m) deep

EATS: small crustaceans, zooplankton, and jellyfish

STATUS:
🍃 unknown

HOW BIG?

6in (15cm) long

Barreleye

The holes at the front look like eyes, but they are really nostrils.

POM-POM ANEMONE

WHERE IN THE WORLD?

LIVES: North Pacific Ocean; up to 13,500ft (4,100m) deep

EATS: plankton

STATUS:
🍃 unknown

HOW BIG?

12in (30cm) wide

Can you see that ball rolling across the muddy ocean floor? The water is giving it a gentle push. The ball is covered in lots of short tentacles. This must be a pom-pom anemone!

Pom-pom anemones can be round or flat. They can also be pink, purple, or white.

Pom-pom anemone

GIANT PHANTOM JELLY

This mysterious, ghostly jellyfish is well hidden in the ocean. Its shades of dark red and brown make it hard to see. You might just catch a glimpse of its large bell and four long arms as it glides by. Don't be surprised to find it's longer than your submarine!

Unlike other jellyfish, the giant phantom jelly doesn't sting. Instead, it traps prey using its long arms.

DON'T MISS!

Keep an eye out for a little fish called the pelagic brotula. It swims close to this jellyfish for protection.

The body, or bell, is very stretchy. It can become four or five times bigger than its normal size when eating prey.

Giant phantom jelly

This jellyfish is a true ocean giant. It is one of the world's largest species of jellyfish.

WHERE IN THE WORLD?

LIVES: all oceans except Arctic; up to 21,600ft (6,600m) deep

EATS: plankton and small fish

STATUS:
🍃 unknown

HOW BIG?

bell 3ft (1m) wide; tentacles 33ft (10m) long

IT'S WILD! It's very rare to spot this jellyfish. It has been seen only about 130 times in more than 100 years.

GIANT OARFISH

Long ago, people called this fish the king of herrings. That's because it looks like it's wearing a crown and often has herrings swimming around it. It was also once thought to be a serpent—a terrifying mythical creature. Today, we know it as the oarfish.

DON'T MISS!

Look out for the oarfish's large, red eggs floating in the water. The female lays millions of them.

A bright red fin runs along the length of the oarfish's back.

The mouth is small and contains no teeth.

This is the world's longest bony fish.

Unlike most fish, the oarfish has no scales on its silvery body. It is covered in slime instead.

Giant oarfish

The oarfish gets its name from the two long fins on the underside of its body. These look like oars.

SEA PIG

WHERE IN THE WORLD?

LIVES: all oceans; 3,300–22,000ft (1,000–6,700m) deep

EATS: dead plants and creatures

STATUS:
🍃 unknown

HOW BIG?

1½–7in (4–17cm) long

Meet the sea pig, a type of sea cucumber. You'll see large groups of these little creatures on the sea floor, rooting around for food.

The legs are used like stilts to stop the body sinking into the soft mud.

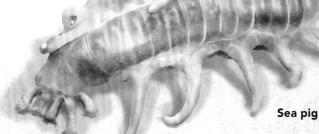

Sea pig

GIANT TUBEWORM

This tubeworm lives in places where few creatures can survive. You'll find it clustered around towers on the seabed where very hot water gushes out.

Each tube is a worm. The white part is the skeleton and the red part is the gills.

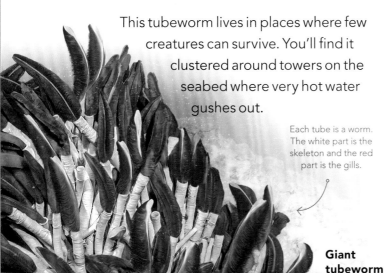

Giant tubeworm

WHERE IN THE WORLD?

LIVES: Pacific Ocean; up to 11,800ft (3,600m) deep

EATS: nothing—bacteria inside the worm make its food

STATUS:
🍃 unknown

HOW BIG?

6½ft (2m) long

CHAMBERED NAUTILUS

WHERE IN THE WORLD?

LIVES: Indo-Pacific; 1,800ft (550m) deep

EATS: fish, crabs, and shrimp

STATUS:
endangered

HOW BIG?

shell 5–9in (12–23cm) wide

Take time to study this beautiful mollusk as it moves around the seabed. First, the chambered nautilus sucks water in to its shell through a tube called a siphon. Then it pumps the water out again at speed to shoot off backward.

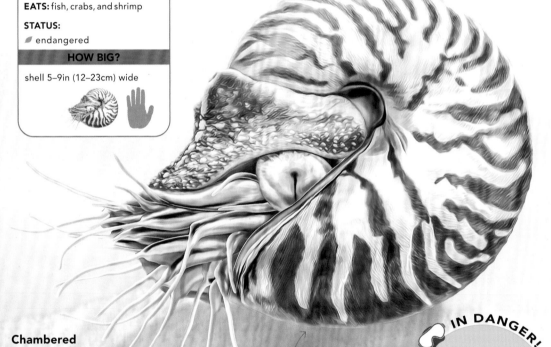

Chambered nautilus

More than 90 tentacles feel for and grab food.

Inside the shell are many sections, or chambers. As the nautilus grows, it builds new chambers to make more room for itself.

IN DANGER!

Too many nautiluses are caught for their pretty shells. Some countries have laws against this.

IT'S WILD! The nautilus has been swimming in the deep ocean for a very long time—even before dinosaurs existed!

EMPEROR DUMBO OCTOPUS

Dumbo octopuses get their name because of the large fins on the sides of their head. These look like the ears of the flying elephant from the Disney film *Dumbo*. You'll see the octopus use these fins for swimming, not flying.

WHERE IN THE WORLD?

LIVES: North Pacific Ocean around Hawaii in USA; 13,000ft (4,000m) deep

EATS: worms and shrimplike crustaceans

STATUS:

🢒 unknown

HOW BIG?

12in (30cm) long

The arms are connected by skin. When the octopus stretches its arms out, they look like a little umbrella.

Dumbo octopuses move slowly by flapping their fins.

SPOTTER FACT

There are 17 types of dumbo octopus. This one was first discovered in 2016 in a very deep part of the ocean.

Emperor dumbo octopus

SPARKS' TWO-ARMED CTENOPHORE

If you met this comb jelly, it would be something very special. Scientists have never seen it with their own eyes. They have only watched it in a video taken by a remote-controlled submarine. Comb jellies, or ctenophores (pronounced *teen-oh-fors*), live in all oceans, but we still don't know very much about this one.

Sparks' two-armed ctenophore

The tiny hairs on the tentacles are called tentilla.

GIANT ISOPOD

WHERE IN THE WORLD?

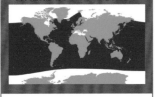

LIVES: Atlantic, Pacific, and Indian oceans; 550–7,000ft (170–2,100m) deep

EATS: dead creatures and marine snow

STATUS:
◣ unknown

HOW BIG?

up to 16in (40cm) long

If you spot this crustacean, watch how it scuffles around on the muddy seabed. It's probably searching for its next meal.

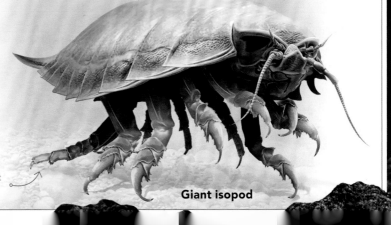

The isopod has 14 jointed legs to help it move across the ocean floor.

Giant isopod

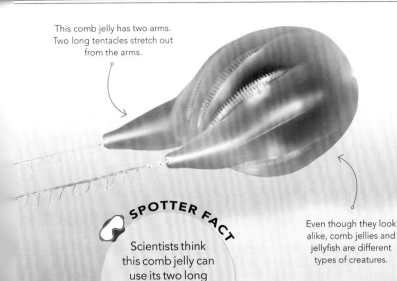

This comb jelly has two arms. Two long tentacles stretch out from the arms.

LIVES: Atlantic Ocean near Puerto Rico; 12,800ft (3,900m) deep

EATS: zooplankton

STATUS:
✎ unknown

HOW BIG?

body up to 3in (8cm) long; tentacles 12–22in (30–56cm) long

SPOTTER FACT

Scientists think this comb jelly can use its two long tentacles to attach itself to the ocean floor.

Even though they look alike, comb jellies and jellyfish are different types of creatures.

BLACK SWALLOWER

You might be surprised to see this creature gulp down a fish that's much bigger than itself. It digests them in its stretchy stomach.

Black swallower

The belly can expand so much that it becomes almost see-though, like a balloon.

LIVES: warm and cool waters; 2,300–8,900ft (700–2,700m) deep

EATS: fish

STATUS:
✎ least concern

HOW BIG?

up to 10in (25cm) long

WHERE IN THE WORLD?

LIVES: Pacific Ocean; 8,200–9,500ft (2,500–2,900m) deep

EATS: plankton

STATUS:
🌱 unknown

HOW BIG?

body 1in (3cm) wide

Dandelion siphonophore

DANDELION SIPHONOPHORE

From far away, this creature looks like a glowing yellow flower. Move closer to see that it's made up of lots of tiny creatures working as one.

The feeding tentacles around it look like a spider's web. They give prey a deadly sting.

WHERE IN THE WORLD?

LIVES: hydrothermal vents in Indian Ocean; 7,800–9,500ft (2,400–2,900m) deep

EATS: ocean chemicals turned into energy

STATUS:
🌱 endangered

HOW BIG?

shell up to 1¾in (4.5cm) long

SCALY-FOOT SNAIL

It's 400°C (750°F) in the hot springs where this snail lives. That's much too hot for a human like you!

The coiled shell is covered with iron. It works like armor plating to protect the snail from the heat.

Scaly-foot snail

E.T. SPONGE

Are you wondering why this deep-sea sponge has such an unusual name? It's because the two holes in its body look like the eyes of the alien from the film *E.T. The Extra-Terrestrial.*

SPOTTER FACT

This sponge lives alongside other strange creatures. Scientists call this area the Forest of the Weird.

Two openings face toward the ocean current and filter bits of food.

This sponge is made of silica—the same material that makes glass. That's why these types of sponges are called glass sponges.

E.T. sponge

The tall stem raises the body to where there is greater flow in the water. Ocean currents bring food the sponge's way.

WHERE IN THE WORLD?

LIVES: Pacific Ocean; 6,500ft (2,000m) deep

EATS: plankton and other tiny creatures

STATUS: unknown

HOW BIG?

at least 8in (20cm) long

WHERE IN THE WORLD?

LIVES: North Pacific Ocean; 1,800–21,600ft (550–6,600m) deep

EATS: shrimp and jellyfish

STATUS:
🍃 least concern

HOW BIG?

up to 8in (21cm) long

OWLFISH

Did you know that big eyes allow animals to see better in the dark? The owlfish needs its enormous eyes to find food and avoid predators in the inky black depths.

DON'T MISS!

Watch how the owlfish escapes the grip of a hungry squid by shedding some of its scales and speeding away.

Owlfish

Compared to its eyes, the owlfish's mouth is tiny. It sucks up shrimp and jellyfish.

WHERE IN THE WORLD?

LIVES: waters in southern hemisphere; 6,500–8,900ft (2,000–2,700m) deep

EATS: crustaceans

STATUS:
🍃 least concern

HOW BIG?

up to 12in (31cm) long

FLABBY WHALEFISH

In the dark, this fish appears black. When it swims in the beam of your submarine lights, you'll see that it's bright red.

Flabby whalefish

This is a female. The male looks nothing like this. Scientists used to think they were two different species.

BLOODYBELLY COMB JELLY

Many comb jellies are see-through, but this one is different. This bloodybelly comb jelly's tummy is always the darkest part of its body. Scientists think this is to hide the bioluminescent creatures it eats. Otherwise, the glow would make the jelly visible to predators, and it could become a meal itself!

WHERE IN THE WORLD?

LIVES: North Pacific Ocean; 820–5,000ft (250–1,500m) deep

EATS: probably zooplankton

STATUS:
🖋 unknown

HOW BIG?

up to 6in (16cm) long

Little hairs called cilia are joined together to form a comb. There are eight rows of combs running along the jelly's body.

The combs move the jelly through the water. As they ripple, they create colorful waves that look like rainbows.

SPOTTER FACT

The bloodybelly comb jelly's scientific name means "brilliant comb."

In the darkest part of the ocean, red appears black. This color makes this jelly almost invisible to other creatures.

Bloodybelly comb jelly

ZOMBIE WORM

Don't mistake this group of worms for a bed of pretty flowers. When a whale dies and sinks to the ocean floor, hordes of zombie worms emerge to feast on its bones.

LIVES: all oceans; up to 13,800ft (4,200m) deep

EATS: fats and protein from animal bones

STATUS: unknown

HOW BIG?

females ¾–3in (2–7cm) long; males are microscopic

Zombie worm

Red plumes absorb oxygen from the water. The worm draws the plumes in if threatened.

Zombie worms dissolve the bones with acid so that they can digest them.

COMMON SAWSHARK

WHERE IN THE WORLD?

LIVES: waters around southern Australia; 130–2,000ft (40–630m) deep

EATS: small fish and crustaceans

STATUS: least concern

HOW BIG?

up to 5ft (1.5m) long

What do you call a shark with a snout that looks like a saw? A sawshark! You won't see this creature cut through rocks or coral. Instead, the sawshark stirs the seabed with its snout to rake up food to eat. If you notice a predator approaching, watch as the sawshark uses its sharp snout to defend itself.

WHERE IN THE WORLD?

LIVES: North Atlantic Ocean; up to 6,500ft (2,000m) deep

EATS: probably plankton

STATUS:
✿ unknown

HOW BIG?

up to 4in (10cm) long

PIGLET SQUID

You can probably guess why the piglet squid was given this name. It has a round body, a wiggly tail, and a tube that looks like a young pig's nose.

Dots on the squid's see-through body form stripes or bands.

Piglet squid

This tube, called a siphon, helps the squid move and breathe.

The snout is one-third of the shark's total length. There are about 20 sharp teeth on each side of it.

Common sawshark

Long feelers, or barbels, help the sawshark find prey buried in the sand.

The top of the body is yellowish to gray-brown with dark blotches. The belly is white.

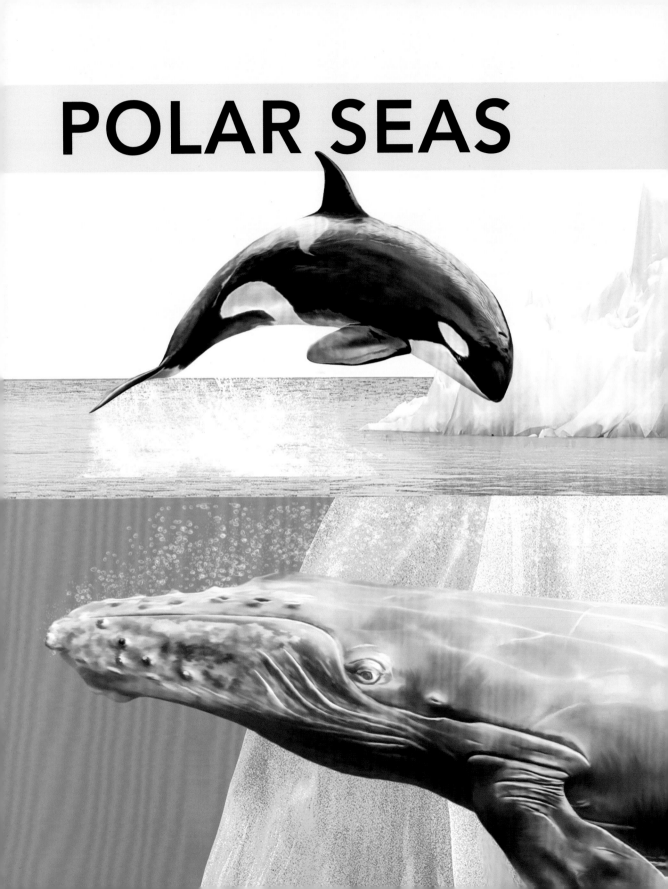

POLAR SEAS

HOW TO SPOT IN POLAR SEAS

The waters around the North and South poles are incredibly cold. They are also full of food—that's why lots of ocean creatures make their homes here. Look out for sea lions and elephant seals, and icefish that never freeze. They all have special ways of keeping warm.

WHAT ARE POLAR SEAS?

THE POLES The waters surrounding the North Pole and the South Pole are known as polar seas.

THE ARCTIC OCEAN The water around the North Pole is called the Arctic Ocean. During the winter months, most of it is frozen into sea ice.

THE SOUTHERN OCEAN At the South Pole is a vast icy continent called Antarctica. It is surrounded by the Southern Ocean.

EXTREME CLIMATE These regions are known for their freezing temperatures, strong winds, and storms.

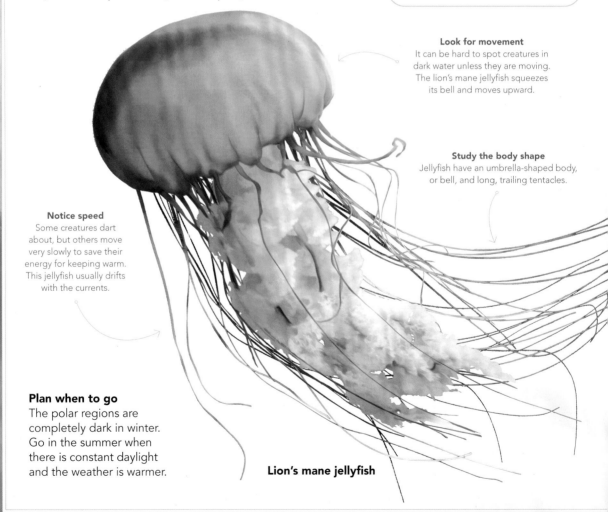

Look for movement
It can be hard to spot creatures in dark water unless they are moving. The lion's mane jellyfish squeezes its bell and moves upward.

Study the body shape
Jellyfish have an umbrella-shaped body, or bell, and long, trailing tentacles.

Notice speed
Some creatures dart about, but others move very slowly to save their energy for keeping warm. This jellyfish usually drifts with the currents.

Plan when to go
The polar regions are completely dark in winter. Go in the summer when there is constant daylight and the weather is warmer.

Lion's mane jellyfish

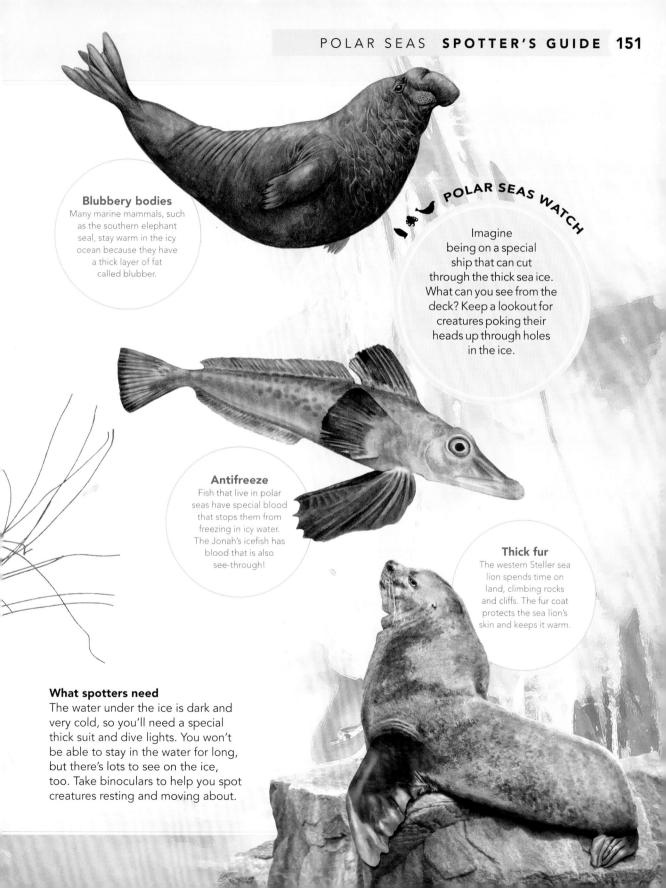

Blubbery bodies
Many marine mammals, such as the southern elephant seal, stay warm in the icy ocean because they have a thick layer of fat called blubber.

POLAR SEAS WATCH

Imagine being on a special ship that can cut through the thick sea ice. What can you see from the deck? Keep a lookout for creatures poking their heads up through holes in the ice.

Antifreeze
Fish that live in polar seas have special blood that stops them from freezing in icy water. The Jonah's icefish has blood that is also see-through!

Thick fur
The western Steller sea lion spends time on land, climbing rocks and cliffs. The fur coat protects the sea lion's skin and keeps it warm.

What spotters need
The water under the ice is dark and very cold, so you'll need a special thick suit and dive lights. You won't be able to stay in the water for long, but there's lots to see on the ice, too. Take binoculars to help you spot creatures resting and moving about.

NARWHAL

It's rare to spot a narwhal—but you won't mistake it for anything else! It has a long, pointy spiral tusk that looks like a unicorn's horn. That's why narwhals are often called the unicorns of the sea. Really, they are a type of whale. Unlike some other whales, narwals don't migrate to warmer waters in winter. Instead, they spend their whole lives in the icy Arctic Ocean.

DON'T MISS!

Look out for holes in the thick ice. You might spot a narwhal or two coming up for air!

Narwhals are mammals. They need to come to the surface to breathe.

SPOTTER FACT

Narwhals live together in large groups called pods. There can be up to 100 narwhals traveling together.

Narwhal

You can tell this narwhal is probably a male because females hardly ever have tusks.

Narwhal's tusk
A tusk is actually a tooth growing outside an animal's mouth. A narwhal's tusk can grow as long as 10ft (3m).

WHERE IN THE WORLD?

LIVES: Arctic Ocean

EATS: fish, squid, and crustaceans

STATUS:
🐟 least concern

HOW BIG?

13–20ft (4–6m) long, excluding the tusk

The skin is darkest when the narwhal is young and fades with age. Old narwhals can be almost completely white.

Scientists think the tusk can help the narwhal find food or a mate.

Narwhals do not have teeth in their mouths. They suck up food and swallow it whole.

Narwhals can dive to more than 4,900ft (1,500m) below the surface.

WALRUS

It's easy to tell which walruses are male and which are female. Male walruses are much larger and have longer tusks. When two males have tusks of the same size, they fight to show the females who's the strongest.

WHERE IN THE WORLD?

LIVES: Arctic Ocean and surrounding coastal waters

EATS: clams, mussels, and fish

STATUS:
vulnerable

HOW BIG?

females 10ft (3m) long;
males up to 12ft (3.7m) long;

Walrus herds
Walruses rest and have their young on land or on ice floes. They live together in big groups called herds.

Walruses have a thick layer of blubber under their skin that keeps them warm. Blubber is a type of fat.

A walrus has up to 700 whiskers on its snout. It uses these to find prey underwater.

IN DANGER!

Global warming is making the ice melt. Walruses have to squeeze onto smaller and smaller ice floes.

Walrus

IT'S WILD! A walrus tusk can grow as long as 3ft (1m) and weigh up to 11lb (5kg).

GREENLAND SHARK

To see this shark, you need to put on your diving suit and jump into the cold water. You can take your time because the Greenland shark swims very slowly—even slower than humans walk on land. It does this to save energy in the freezing waters of its Arctic home. This shark grows slowly, too. It increases in length by just ½in (1cm) per year.

A Greenland shark can live until it is around 400 years old. It is the longest-living vertebrate in the world.

This type of shark has a small head with a short snout. Like many sharks, it is more or less blind.

The Greenland shark is part of the family of sleeper sharks.

Greenland shark

SPOTTER FACT

A female Greenland shark is ready to have pups when she is about 150 years old.

WHERE IN THE WORLD?

LIVES: Arctic and North Atlantic oceans

EATS: fish, squid, seabirds, seals, and other marine mammals

STATUS:
vulnerable

HOW BIG?

13–16ft (4–5m) long

Polar bear family

Polar bears usually have two cubs at a time. The cubs stay with their mother for about two years, learning to hunt, eat, and swim.

DON'T MISS!

A polar bear has black skin underneath its white fur. Scientists think this helps it to absorb the sun's warmth.

POLAR BEAR

You'll need a keen eye to spot this snow-white bear moving about on the ice because its white fur means it is well camouflaged. The male is the biggest bear in the world, weighing up to 1,900lb (800kg). Huge paws spread its weight when it's walking on thin ice. They also help the bear power through the water when it's swimming.

When it's diving, the polar bear closes its nostrils to stop water from entering.

IT'S WILD! An adult male polar bear can be more than 10ft (3m) tall when standing on its hind legs.

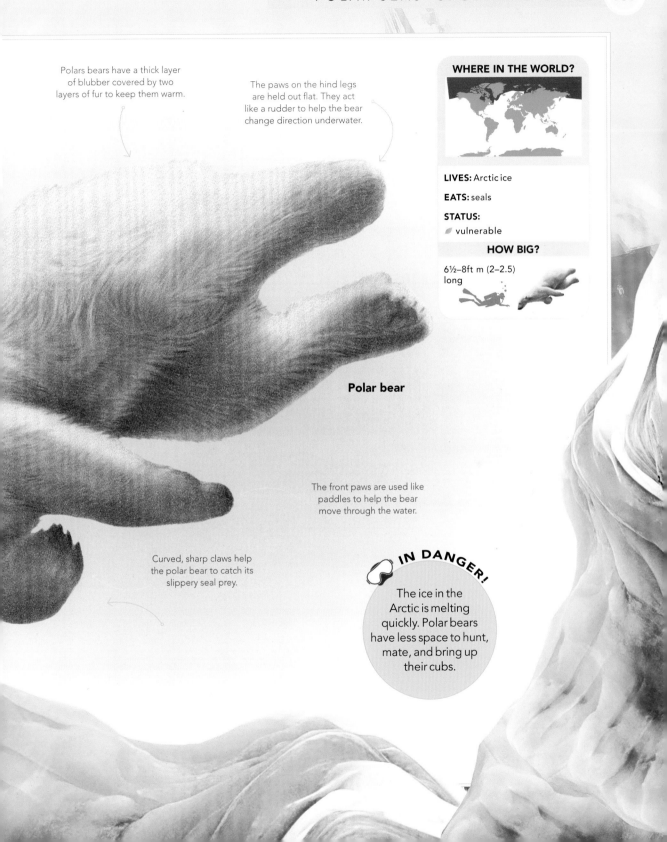

Polars bears have a thick layer of blubber covered by two layers of fur to keep them warm.

The paws on the hind legs are held out flat. They act like a rudder to help the bear change direction underwater.

WHERE IN THE WORLD?

LIVES: Arctic ice

EATS: seals

STATUS: vulnerable

HOW BIG?

6½–8ft m (2–2.5) long

Polar bear

The front paws are used like paddles to help the bear move through the water.

Curved, sharp claws help the polar bear to catch its slippery seal prey.

IN DANGER!

The ice in the Arctic is melting quickly. Polar bears have less space to hunt, mate, and bring up their cubs.

BELUGA WHALE

Can you hear chirping, whistling, and squeaking? It's not a bird making these noises, but a beluga whale. The belugas use these songlike sounds to talk to each other. This is why they are also called the canaries of the sea.

Belugas are unlike other whales because they can move their heads from side to side.

Belugas are born gray or brown and become white as they grow up. The white color helps them blend in with the sea ice.

Almost half of the beluga's body is blubber, a thick layer of fat that keeps it warm.

Belugas normally live together in a group of five to 25. The group is called a pod.

SPOTTER FACT
The beluga makes clicking sounds to find food and navigate. The bump on its head makes these clicks louder.

Beluga whale

IT'S WILD! A beluga can dive to around 3,000ft (900m) and stay there for at least 20 minutes.

STELLER SEA LION

What's that roaring so loudly? Look, a huge male Steller sea lion has hauled himself out of the water and is sitting on the rocks. The females give birth to their pups here. The males protect them by bellowing and bobbing their heads up and down. This is their way of telling other males to stay away.

Steller sea lions have big heads. The male's snout is flatter than the female's.

The male is three times as heavy as the female. His broad neck and shoulders are covered with a thick mane of fur.

DON'T MISS!

Look out for this sea lion walking across land with its back flippers turned forward like feet.

Powerful front flippers help the sea lion move through water. The Steller sea lion's top swimming speed is 17mph (27kmph).

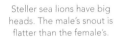

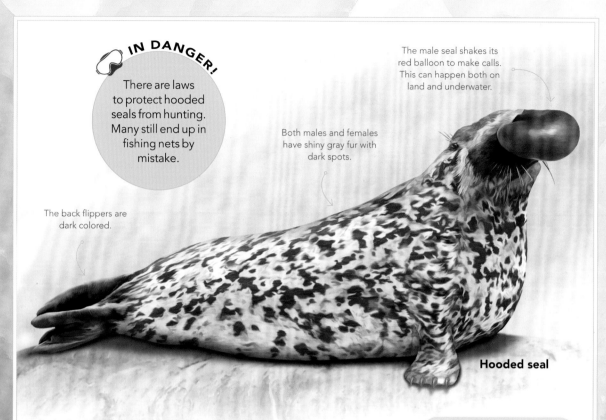

IN DANGER!

There are laws to protect hooded seals from hunting. Many still end up in fishing nets by mistake.

The male seal shakes its red balloon to make calls. This can happen both on land and underwater.

Both males and females have shiny gray fur with dark spots.

The back flippers are dark colored.

Hooded seal

HOODED SEAL

You can't mistake a hooded seal, because of the strange-looking red balloon on its nose. It's only the male that has it. When he wants to impress female hooded seals, this balloonlike sac drops down from his nose. He then blows air into it to inflate it. The hooded seal is an expert swimmer. When it needs to escape a predator, the seal uses its front flippers to haul itself out of the water. It wriggles across land on its belly.

WHERE IN THE WORLD?

LIVES: cold waters of North Atlantic and Arctic oceans

EATS: fish, squid, sea stars, mussels, and crustaceans

STATUS:
vulnerable

HOW BIG?

6½–8ft (2–2.5m) long

IT'S WILD! Hooded seals spend most of their lives in water. They can live for up to 35 years.

WHERE IN THE WORLD?

LIVES: Arctic Ocean

EATS: small crustaceans and fish

STATUS:
 least concern

HOW BIG?

10in (25cm) long

POLAR COD

You'll easily come across this fish, as it's very common in the Arctic Ocean. You won't be able to stand the chilly water for long, but it's no problem for the polar cod. It has special chemicals in its body to stop it from freezing.

The top side of the polar cod's gray-brown body is covered in small, dark dots.

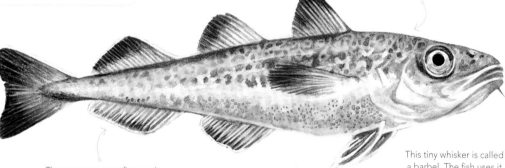

This tiny whisker is called a barbel. The fish uses it to search for food in the dark water.

There are two gray fins on the belly and three on the back, each separate from the other.

Polar cod

A polar cod sometimes swims with others. This group of fish is called a school.

SPOTTER FACT

The polar cod is a favorite meal for seals, walruses, narwhals, beluga whales, and seabirds.

HUMPBACK WHALE

Your best chance of seeing a humpback whale is when it comes to the surface to eat. It opens its mouth wide and swallows lots of water containing thousands of tiny creatures called krill. This little crustacean lives near the ocean surface, along with tens of thousands of others. Humpback whales travel to the polar seas especially to find this food.

The hump on its back gives this whale its name.

Each tail fluke has its own pattern on the underside, making it easy to tell one whale from another.

Male humpbacks are spectacular singers. They sing the same song again and again.

WHERE IN THE WORLD?

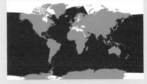

LIVES: all oceans

EATS: small crustaceans (mostly krill) and small fish

STATUS:
🍃 least concern

HOW BIG?

up to 60ft (18m) long

DON'T MISS!

Listen out for a "whup" sound. Scientists believe this is the whales saying hello to each other.

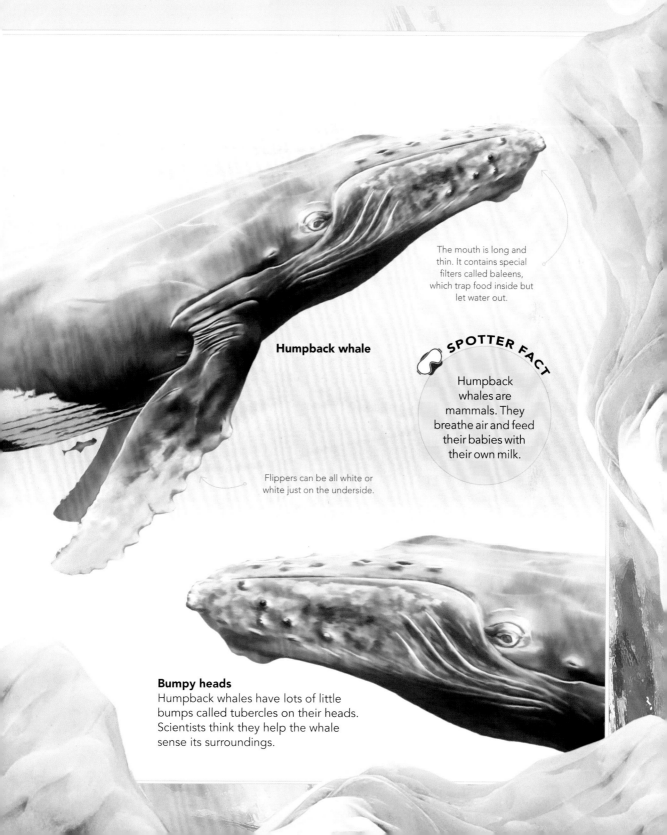

The mouth is long and thin. It contains special filters called baleens, which trap food inside but let water out.

Humpback whale

SPOTTER FACT

Humpback whales are mammals. They breathe air and feed their babies with their own milk.

Flippers can be all white or white just on the underside.

Bumpy heads
Humpback whales have lots of little bumps called tubercles on their heads. Scientists think they help the whale sense its surroundings.

EMPEROR PENGUIN

Can you see a big bird standing tall on the ice? The mighty emperor penguin lives in the coldest place on Earth—Antarctica. Like all penguins, the emperor has wings but it can't fly. Instead, its wings help the penguin speed through the icy ocean as it hunts for food.

The hook at the end of the beak helps the penguin grab food.

The emperor penguin is the largest of the 19 penguin species.

Two layers of feathers and a lot of body fat help the penguin to stay warm.

Emperor penguin

Emperor penguins have strong claws on their feet for gripping the ice.

DON'T MISS!
Spot these streamlined birds as they scoot around in the water. They use their feet and tail as a rudder.

IT'S WILD! Photos taken from space have shown new penguin colonies on the vast Antarctic continent.

SPOTTER FACT

Penguins live together in large groups called colonies. There are 66 known colonies in Antarctica.

WHERE IN THE WORLD?

LIVES: Antarctica

EATS: fish, krill, and squid

STATUS:
near threatened

HOW BIG?

up to 4ft (1.2m) long

Expert divers

Emperor penguins are the deepest divers of all birds. They can reach depths of more than 1,800ft (550m) and stay underwater for up to 20 minutes at a time before they need to come up for air.

JONAH'S ICEFISH

A Jonah's icefish will spot you before you spot it, as it can see really well in the dark water under the ice. Climb in a submarine if you want to look at this fish's nest. Males collect stones and arrange them in a circle on the seabed. After the females lay their eggs, the males guard the nest to keep the eggs safe from predators.

WHERE IN THE WORLD?

LIVES: Southern Ocean

EATS: fish and krill

STATUS:
◢ unknown

HOW BIG?

22in (56cm) long

The top and front fins are big and black. They stand out from the body.

Big eyes let the maximum amount of light in. This helps the fish to see in the dark.

DON'T MISS!

Search the seabed for a huge colony of icefish nests. Scientists think there could be at least 60 million nests.

Jonah's icefish

The long head makes the icefish look a bit like a crocodile.

Special nests
Icefish nests look almost like works of art. Male icefish carefully push small stones into a circle about 30in (75cm) wide. Then the female lays at least 1,700 fish eggs inside.

LION'S MANE JELLYFISH

Don't get too close! The huge lion's mane jellyfish has up to 1,200 long, trailing tentacles. These give a nasty sting, which stuns fish and other prey. Like other jellyfish, the lion's mane is almost completely made of water. Just five percent is solid.

WHERE IN THE WORLD?

LIVES: cold waters (including Arctic Ocean)

EATS: zooplankton, small fish, crustaceans, comb jellies, and other jellyfish

STATUS:
🖋 unknown

HOW BIG?

120ft (36.5m) long

A jellyfish's body is called a bell.

The jellyfish's mouth is underneath the bell.

Small fish hide under the lion's mane's bell to protect themselves from other predators.

SPOTTER FACT

This jellyfish lives in very deep waters where there is no light. It can glow in the dark to lure prey.

Lion's mane jellyfish

The flowing tentacles look like a lion's mane, which gives the jellyfish its name.

The thicker tentacles are called oral arms. They pull prey into the jellyfish's mouth.

IT'S WILD! The lion's mane jellyfish is the largest jellyfish in the world. Its tentacles can grow more than 98 ft (30m) long.

WHERE IN THE WORLD?

LIVES: Antarctica and islands in South Atlantic and Indian oceans

EATS: mainly krill, but also other crustaceans, small fish, and squid

STATUS:
 vulnerable

HOW BIG?

20–28in (50–70cm) long

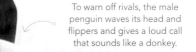

MACARONI PENGUIN

Imagine having a hairstyle as fabulous as this penguin's! Yellow crest feathers stick out of its black head. It's called a macaroni penguin, but it has nothing to do with pasta. A long time ago, *macaroni* meant "a stylish man who wears feathers in his hat."

This type of penguin has a big orange beak and red eyes.

To warn off rivals, the male penguin waves its head and flippers and gives a loud call that sounds like a donkey.

Macaroni penguins can waddle, jump, and climb across cliffs and rocks.

When it's swimming, the penguin uses its long tail like a rudder to steer where it wants to go.

Macaroni penguin

IN DANGER!

Conservationists are helping to protect macaroni penguins on the islands where they live and breed.

ANTARCTIC SILVERFISH

You might glimpse these shimmering fish as they swim from the sunlit surface to the chilly, dark depths. Antarctic silverfish don't freeze, even when the water around them turns to ice. They have a special type of blood that stops ice crystals from forming in their bodies.

WHERE IN THE WORLD?

LIVES: Southern Ocean

EATS: krill and other crustaceans and marine worms

STATUS:
🦐 least concern

HOW BIG?

6in (15cm) long

The fin on its back is darker than the other fins.

A slender body allows the Antarctic silverfish to swim quickly and easily.

Antarctic silverfish

SPOTTER FACT

This fish lives in the open ocean. It is an important food for seals, penguins, and whales.

The female lays her eggs in sea ice. When the fish hatch, they stay near the ice until they are big enough to swim away.

Antarctic silverfish grow very slowly. They breed for the first time when they are seven to nine years old.

ORCA

Watch this orca jump out of the water and high into the air. What an incredible acrobat! Leaping through the air is the quickest way for the orca to get closer to its prey. Orcas hunt in teams. They work together to herd prey or to separate one from its group.

Orcas are mostly black on top with white patches underneath.

An orca swims very fast when hunting. It's the second-fastest marine mammal after the common dolphin.

Orca

Orcas have a white patch above their eyes. The shape of it is different for each creature. Researchers take photos of the eye patch to tell orcas apart.

Spyhopping

Orcas sometimes poke their heads out of the water to see if there is food nearby—perhaps a seal resting on an ice floe. This is called spyhopping.

A group of orcas is called a pod. It is often made up of different families.

SPOTTER FACT

Orcas stay close to their mothers all their lives. They even live with their grandmothers.

Orcas are the largest members of the dolphin family. They are also called killer whales.

WHERE IN THE WORLD?

LIVES: worldwide, including Arctic and Southern oceans

EATS: fish, squid, sharks, rays, penguins, seals, whales, sea turtles, and seabirds

STATUS:
🌿 unknown

HOW BIG?

16–26ft (5–8m) long

SOUTHERN ELEPHANT SEAL

The huge southern elephant seal stays warm in the freezing waters of Antarctica because of all the fat in its body. Don't be surprised if you see it hunting all day long. To get this fat, the southern elephant seal has to eat lots of fish and squid.

WHERE IN THE WORLD?

LIVES: Southern Ocean and surrounding waters

EATS: fish and squid

STATUS:
least concern

HOW BIG?

females 6½–10ft (2–3m) long; males 13–20ft (4–6m) long

This seal is a deep diver. It can dive thousands of feet down before it needs to come up for air.

The southern elephant seal spends about 10 months per year hunting in the ocean.

The southern elephant seal is the biggest of all the seal species. A male can weigh more than 4 tons.

The nose of the male seal looks like an elephant's trunk.

DON'T MISS!

In the breeding season, watch as the males fight each other over which female to mate with.

Southern elephant seal

GIANT ANTARCTIC OCTOPUS

You'll need to turn on the headlights of your submarine to spot this octopus. It usually lives in deep water where there's no sunlight. There are several different types of octopus in the Southern Ocean. Some are small and some are large. The giant Antarctic octopus is the largest of them all. It lives here and nowhere else.

WHERE IN THE WORLD?

LIVES: Southern Ocean

EATS: brittle stars, fish, crustaceans, mollusks, and marine worms

STATUS:
least concern

HOW BIG?

mantle 11in (28cm) long; total 35in (90cm) long

The giant Antarctic octopus has only one row of suckers on its arms. Most other octopuses have two rows.

Giant Antarctic octopus

All octopuses have eight arms. The giant Antarctic octopus's arms are two to three times longer than its body..

DON'T MISS!
Watch the giant Antarctic octopus as it hunts. It uses venom in its saliva to paralyze or kill larger prey.

IT'S WILD! This octopus can drill through the hard shells of prey and inject venom through the hole.

INDEX